"We were very fortunate to have Dr Laurie provide us with the guidance on how to help our son, who was diagnosed with ASD when he was very young. Dr Laurie was there whenever we were faced with challenges related to ASD. *College on the Autism Spectrum* is an invaluable resource and must-read for parents who have a college-bound child with ASD. Dr Laurie's knowledge of the college environment helped our son navigate through the complex process and get the help he needed to successfully graduate college."

—*JoAnn Mendonca, alumni parent of Dr Laurie's Friends Program*

"Laurie has been working with high functioning children and adolescents on the autism spectrum and their families for 28 years and her experience and wisdom have contributed to writing a highly recommended guide for parents. This guide will encourage the mental health and wellbeing of the college student who has autism as well as their parents."

—*Tony Attwood, Minds & Hearts Clinic, Brisbane*

"Dr Leventhal-Belfer writes an indispensable guide for preparing children with autistic spectrum disorder going to college. Her years of experience and close connections with patient families lead to clear and concise recommendations for parents. Dr Leventhal-Belfer shares a detailed and nuanced knowledge of the specific opportunities and requirements for obtaining academic and general accommodations through the university."

—*Dr Michael F. Haberecht, staff psychiatrist, Vaden Health Center, Stanford University*

D1202666

"This book can truly serve as a lifesaving guide for parents of individuals with ASD who are getting ready to embark on the scary journey of sending their child to college. Frank advice, from parents, individuals with ASD, and therapist is provided, offering easy strategies for greatest success."

—*Cheryl Klaiman, PhD, Associate Professor and Director of Diagnostic Services, Marcus Autism Center and Emory University School of Medicine*

College on the Autism Spectrum

of related interest

Parties, Dorms and Social Norms
A Crash Course in Safe Living for Young Adults on the Autism Spectrum
Lisa M. Meeks and Tracy Loye Masterson with
Michelle Rigler and Emily Quinn
Illustrated by Amy Rutherford
ISBN 978 1 84905 746 2
eISBN 978 1 78450 192 1

Successful Social Articles into Adulthood
Growing Up with Social Stories¨
Dr Siobhan Timmins
Foreword by Carol Gray
ISBN 978 1 78592 138 4
eISBN 978 1 78450 403 8

First Class Support for College Students on the Autism Spectrum
Practical Advice for College Counselors and Educators
Michael W. Duggan
ISBN 978 1 78592 413 2
eISBN 978 1 78450 777 0

Teaching University Students with Autism Spectrum Disorder
A Guide to Developing Academic Capacity and Proficiency
Kimberley McMahon-Coleman and Kim Draisma
ISBN 978 1 84905 420 1
eISBN 978 0 85700 798 8

Developing College Skills in Students with Autism and Asperger's Syndrome
Sarita Freedman
ISBN 978 1 84310 917 4
eISBN 978 0 85700 292 1

College on the Autism Spectrum

A Parent's Guide to Students' Mental Health and Wellbeing

Laurie Leventhal-Belfer

Foreword by Tony Attwood

Jessica Kingsley Publishers
London and Philadelphia

First published in 2020
by Jessica Kingsley Publishers
73 Collier Street
London N1 9BE, UK
and
400 Market Street, Suite 400
Philadelphia, PA 19106, USA

www.jkp.com

Library of Congress Cataloging in Publication Data
A CIP catalog record for this book is available from the Library of Congress

British Library Cataloguing in Publication Data
A CIP catalogue record for this book is available from the British Library

ISBN 978 1 78592 593 1
eISBN 978 1 78592 596 2

Printed and bound in the United States

Contents

Foreword

One of the diagnostic characteristics of autism is insistence on sameness, with considerable anxiety and distress when established routines are changed. Starting college inevitably involves new daily routines, expectations and social conventions.

There are clearly positive aspects of going to college; for example, the opportunity to make new friends, potentially a reduction in bullying and rejection by peers, the enjoyment of intellectual stimulation and accomplishments, and perceived freedom from parental micromanaging. However, there are potential challenges too, which are often of great concern for parents. These include coping with daily living skills, facing a range of temptations and distractions, adapting to new social and academic conventions, and managing stress and anxiety.

During the high school years, a parent may have provided considerable support in the areas of time management, nutrition, budgeting, personal hygiene, and sleep. That parent may have been so efficient in facilitating daily living skills that the student was not aware of their support needs, failing to recognize the cues that indicate a particular requirement, such as having a shower. A parent may have provided regular daily monitoring, prompts, guidance, and reassurance that are unavailable once the student leaves home for college. It is imperative, therefore, that increasing independence in daily living skills becomes a part of home life some years before going to college.

There are many temptations and distractions at college: for example, the opportunity to indulge in increasing, unsupervised screen time; the lure of intoxication by both legal (alcohol) and illegal drugs (e.g., marijuana); and the possibility of developing romantic and sexual relationships, inherently distracting and unsettling for a vulnerable young person. A typical student will have friends at college to provide advice and emotional support, but the student who has autism may not easily establish a trustworthy social network of people to whom they can disclose their thoughts and feelings.

While the student may tend towards reclusiveness, there is obvious advantage in having friends and acquaintances with whom to discuss assignments, provide support in potentially risky situations, and even develop romantic relationships. They should be encouraged, therefore, to initiate social interactions with fellow students on their course, and to seek out and join some of the many college groups and societies in areas of talent or interest, such as choral singing, music, or drama, to name but a few.

There will be new social conventions and expectations at college. These are often fairly obvious for a typical student, but less so for the student who has autism, who may need guidance in the social aspects of college life with fellow students and academic staff. They may be less aware of social conventions, sometimes appearing to be politically incorrect, or being perceived as having extreme political, social, or religious beliefs. There may also be a risk of their being recruited by extremist student groups.

Because of the many potential pitfalls in this unfamiliar student life, a number of colleges are developing a buddy system for students who have autism. The buddy may simply be a fellow student who wants to help someone who has autism, or perhaps a fellow senior student who has autism themselves. The intention is that they meet regularly to discuss and provide support on a range of college issues, from developing friendships to assignments and exam preparations. In Australia, several colleges are starting Neurodiversity Hubs, providing a meeting place and mutual support for neurodiverse students. In other colleges, a student who has autism is allocated a buddy who is a graduate student of clinical psychology at the college. The student psychologist can provide support with regard to friendships and social conventions, as well as emotional support. This can be in addition to the college's disability support and mental health services.

There are also social conventions and protocols associated with academic college life. The student who has autism may have an intolerance of uncertainty and ambiguity, with difficulty accepting an alternative perspective, and during tutorials may talk too much or too little. There can also be a tendency for the student to correct publicly the professor's errors, which will not endear them to the academic staff.

As much as the student who has autism will need guidance in the social culture and codes of behavior and conduct at college, the academic staff will also need training and guidance in how to facilitate the inclusion of a student who has autism in their classes and tutorials.

Another area that requires attention when a young person with autism starts college is that of stress and emotion management. During the high school years, parents would have been able to accurately "read" the subtle signs of increasing stress or mood disorder in their adolescent son or daughter, even when the young person may not have been cognitively aware of these signs. The parents would have been able to suggest strategies for stress and emotion management; but at college, where there may be no one to closely monitor stress levels and emotional wellbeing, the risk is that increasing stress may develop into or exacerbate an anxiety disorder, or the student may slowly sink into severe depression. Student support services will need to elicit from the student themselves (or the student's parents) the personal indicators of increasing stress and worsening mood, as well as monitoring increasing social isolation and any interpersonal friction. The support services will need to have a regular and frequent schedule of meetings with the student to review stress and emotion levels, as well as academic progress.

A source of stress for a student who has autism can be the sensory and social aspects of college. There may be sensitivity to specific sounds, light intensity, and aromas. The college may need to recognize this characteristic of autism and make accommodations and compromises. Another source of stress is the sheer number of students in lecture halls and on campus, which can be overwhelming for the student with autism. A simple solution for this can be for the student to arrive at the lecture hall early, when it is still relatively quiet, and select a seat that is slightly more secluded and near the exit. A more extreme, but less satisfactory, solution is for the student with autism to complete the course externally on the Internet. While this enables the student to avoid lecture halls and crowded campuses entirely, the disadvantage is the lack of opportunity to meet fellow students on campus, make friends, and engage in face-to-face conversations with other students and lecturers.

There may need to be specific help with exams, which are a great source of anxiety for students who have autism. Accommodations can include avoiding a large examination hall by taking the exam in an adjacent small room; being able to type rather than write exam answers (autism is associated with dysgraphia); and, at the start of the examination, a member of staff being available to ensure the student has not taken a too literal interpretation of the exam question.

Another source of stress is the requirement to submit a group project or assignment. The student who has autism will need guidance and support in several aspects of group work. These may include identifying and joining a group; when and how to contribute to group discussion (not being dictatorial or subservient); coping with criticisms (and compliments); and recognition and acceptance of the possibility that there may be an uneven distribution of the workload between group members.

When the student with autism becomes stressed, there may be a tendency for them to become rigid in their thinking, and to catastrophize. Thus, they may easily take offence, misinterpret others' intentions, or clash with lecturers or tutors, particularly regarding marking and grades. There can be a dramatic over-reaction to conflict or disappointment, with a highly emotional student choosing to quit the course. In these circumstances, there will need to be an adjudicator who understands the characteristics of autism in order to achieve reconciliation and calmly review decisions made "in the heat of the moment."

But, despite all the challenges regarding college life for the student who has autism, it is important for colleges to recognize that autism is also associated with many positive features. Students with autism often demonstrate an original way of thinking and problem-solving; they have an ability to determine patterns (and pattern breaks); they show remarkable attention to detail; and they exhibit great determination to strive for excellence. In short, the student with autism could be one of the college's most illustrious graduates and prize winners.

Tony Attwood

Dedication

This book is dedicated to the kids and parents who participated in The Friends Program, my therapeutic group program for young children with Asperger's Disorder.

Over the years, I heard from these parents when their children were being bullied, did not qualify for an Individual Education Plan (IEP), had trouble making friends, or needed additional support because of difficulties in middle and high school. The parents of these children have taught me how complex and diverse they are. They kept me updated as the children entered different stages of their lives, and shared their fears, challenges, disappointments, and pride in the children's progress.

I often heard from them again as they became increasingly anxious about their teens' upcoming transition and adaptation to college. Their struggles and triumphs inspired my interest in writing a book to make the journey easier for future ASD (Autism Spectrum Disorder) college students.

The kids and parents whose stories are included in this book had the same goal of easing the transition for others. I want to thank each of them for their candor and invaluable insights.

I also want to thank my colleagues who have supported me along the way, in particular Wendy Froehlich-Santino for her guidance in making sure that the book covered the issues and laws that pertain to students who are taking prescription medication. And I want to thank my editors, Kay Paumier and Andrea Grindeland, for their editorial skills, support, and empathy for the reader.

Lastly, I want to thank Jessie and Rose for their inspirational idea for the cover, and my husband, Howard, who has stood by me and helped me as I traveled the ups and downs of writing books that capture the passion I feel towards my work and the families I serve.

Preface

This book is for parents of children on the Spectrum who are either preparing to apply to college or are just starting their college years.

Some of these children may have rejected their diagnosis and successfully managed high school with minimal support. Others understood their needs and did well in high school with support from a tutor, their school, their therapist and, of course, their parents. Whatever the circumstance, when a child goes to college, the parents will not be there to support them when they feel overwhelmed, disagree with a teacher, or wonder why they are not included in social events.

Over the years I have received many phone calls from parents desperate for advice about how to help their child who was "crashing" during the freshman year in college. These devoted parents had worked hard to foster their child's success in school. However, their child still struggled with the increased demands of college. These parents were not prepared for their child's decision to play online games or gamble rather than seek help with their classes. They were shocked to learn that they could not set up services for their child at college, and that they could not communicate directly with the mental health or disability center due to privacy regulations. This book is designed to provide parents of high-functioning children on the Spectrum with a guide to the college experience, including how to set up a good support network, find the right university, and access resources to help their child's mental health and social wellbeing.

Chapter 1

Being on the Spectrum

Today more and more high-functioning children on the Spectrum are being accepted into college, and then going on to have productive careers. This is promising. However, students on the Spectrum face myriad new academic and social challenges in college, which can adversely affect their school experience, and their mental, emotional, and physical wellbeing.

The fact that you've picked up this book suggests that you are the parent or guardian of a child "on the Spectrum" who is going to college, or is there now.

And the fact that you and your child have made it to this point is a testament to how special both of you are. Your support has made this achievement possible.

However, like any college student, your child is entering a world with new challenges and new possibilities. They will have the added challenge of being on the Spectrum and away from the familiar support systems that have served them so well.

Most of this book will focus on how you can help your child on the Spectrum succeed in college. Before we get into the practical aspects of dealing with college life, we will take a look at some basic considerations.

Specifically, in this chapter we will look at the following:

- On the Spectrum: Autism Spectrum Disorder (ASD)

- understanding the diagnosis

- is support really needed?

- overcoming the diagnosis obstacle

- The Friends Program

- how you can help

On the Spectrum: Autism Spectrum Disorder (ASD)

Adolescence is not easy for anyone. A growing body of literature describes how the adolescent brain acquires new skills and experiences "cognitive disequilibrium" as the mind and body grow. In fact, the brain is not completely mature until someone is in their late 20s. Adolescents do not have fully mature judgment or optimal decision-making skills, increasing the risk of adverse events such as accidental injuries, violent behavior and unintended pregnancies (Siegel 2013). So, adolescence is rough enough without being on the Spectrum.

To manage the challenges of being on the Spectrum, students need to understand the diagnosis and realize that their symptoms, which may have been manageable during high school, will likely be more acute under the stress of college life. This self-awareness and acceptance are key to unlocking the services that can support their success and wellbeing at college.

Understanding the diagnosis

In 2013, the American Psychiatric Association's *Diagnostic and Statistical Manual of Mental Disorders* (*DSM-5*) created the diagnosis of ASD by merging the diagnoses of autism, PDD-NOS (pervasive developmental disorder – not otherwise specified), and Asperger's Syndrome into one. While therapists and other professionals who work with ASD kids understand the different levels of functionality of ASD patients, many high-functioning kids and their parents have difficulty accepting the new diagnosis of ASD. They feel that it does not differentiate them enough from students with more severe academic, developmental, and behavioral issues (Leventhal-Belfer 2013).

> One young adult who was previously diagnosed with Asperger's said he was uncomfortable with the new ASD diagnosis as he felt that it encompassed too wide a range of individuals. "I personally have an issue with them clumping it all together. I definitely feel that I do not have autism; but I do have Asperger's. It's a higher form of a higher condition. I would rather be considered to have straight-up Asperger's."
> Steve

As imperfect as the new diagnosis may be, you and your child need to understand and accept it because it is essential to getting support services at college. And those services can dramatically impact your child's academic and social success.

NOTE

Being "on the Spectrum" is clinically known as Autism Spectrum Disorder or ASD. However, many parents and children prefer to say that they are "on the Spectrum." So, throughout this book, I use Autism Spectrum Disorder or the acronym ASD when discussing diagnosis, research, and services, and "on the Spectrum" when focusing on more general issues.

Is support really needed?

To gain a better understanding of the amount and type of help your child might need at college, think about how you presently support your child.

Do you:

- help your child wake up?
- prepare breakfast?
- drive him or her to school?

Does your child have:

- a tutor?
- a therapist?

Does your child:

- help around the house?
- manage his or her own money?
- manage his or her schedule?
- meet school deadlines without assistance?
- communicate needs directly with his or her tutor, counselor or therapist?
- manage his or her medications?

Do you:

- "patrol" schoolwork?
- help with homework?
- remind your child about school deadlines?
- set up appointments with therapists and tutors?

- drive your child to medical appointments or other obligations?

- cook, clean, and manage your child's laundry?

This list could go on and on. The idea here is to honestly assess how much help your child needed in high school. Then consider that he or she will probably need all this support—and more—at college, and that you won't be there to help. Hopefully, the process of answering these questions helps you to better understand the importance of college support services.

And here's the tricky part: you cannot request services for them. At 18 your child will legally be an adult and will therefore need to apply for support services on their own. They will also have to make their own appointments to see physicians, therapists, counselors, and the like.

Getting these services requires that your child accepts the diagnosis.

Overcoming the diagnosis obstacle

Unfortunately, many students on the Spectrum do not thrive in college because they refuse to accept their diagnosis, which prevents them from getting services that would help them navigate the campus, manage their schedule, receive accommodations for tests and papers, and get mental health support or peer counseling.

Often these young adults have been bullied in elementary, middle, or high school, and they associate bullying with the fact that they received services. More likely the main trigger for the bullying was because they displayed atypical behavior or shared their diagnosis with kids who didn't understand the condition, in a system that did not protect them from bullying. They fear that sharing their diagnosis at college will result in being ostracized or bullied again.

Interestingly, these students often recognize that their parents, therapists, teachers, tutors, and/or medication significantly helped them get accepted to college in the first place. Nevertheless, that recognition isn't always enough to overcome the perceived stigma of the diagnosis.

However, the decision not to share their diagnosis with the school has a cost. I have seen many students who chose not to disclose their diagnosis become anxious and depressed. The added social and academic stresses of college caused recurrent problems that were not addressed because the teen refused support services.

Reasons many students do not share the diagnosis at college

It's not enough for you as a parent to accept the diagnosis, your child must understand and accept it as well. Here are some of the most common reasons many students resist asking for services and some sample responses you can use.

REASON 1

No one will believe that I have ASD. It isn't the right diagnosis for me anyway.

A possible response

Diagnoses are imperfect, and ASD is no different. However, the diagnosis is an important tool for helping to secure help you need now, as well as services you may need in the future. Professionals know there are distinct levels within the ASD diagnosis, and that you are at the high-functioning end of the Spectrum. It will be up to you to decide who you share the diagnosis with at school. As you probably saw in high school, most of your teachers forget that you have an IEP (Individual Education Plan) when you do well academically.

REASON 2

I don't need help. I don't want special services. I made it through high school without them.

A possible response

These services are not designed to give you an advantage over other students, but rather to level the playing field so that you're not at a disadvantage. As for whether you need services, you may have been fine in high school, but the course work in college will be more demanding. Plus, you will need to take care of your day-to-day living—deadlines, schedule, food, laundry, money, health, transportation, and more—without the support you had at home. Most ASD students who quit college do so mainly because of the stress from managing day-to-day life and social interactions with their peers, not because of academic challenges.

REASON 3

I don't want people to treat me differently.

A possible response

You don't need to share your diagnosis with any of your peers, but having a diagnosis will help you get the services you need. Academically, the diagnosis allows you to get accommodations such as more time to complete a test, the chance to take tests in different formats (e.g., written instead of oral, essay instead of multiple choice), and the option to have a note-taker or tutor. The diagnosis can also open the door for mental health and other services. Granted, getting a diagnosis doesn't guarantee you will get these accommodations and services, but without a diagnosis it is difficult to secure this extra help.

Another consideration is that in sharing your diagnosis you're helping to educate others on what it means to be on the Spectrum. Keep in mind, a growing number of colleges and universities provide specific programs for ASD students. (See Chapter 2 for advice on selecting the right college and Chapter 6 for more information on getting services.)

REASON 4
My professors will be annoyed if they have to accommodate me.

A possible response
Your professor may be cranky, but this isn't your fault. Making these accommodations is part of their job and something they will get used to doing not just for you, but for other students with similar needs as well. If you feel your professor is treating you unfairly because of the accommodation request, bring this to the attention of the disabilities office.

If your child is still worried about being associated with the ASD diagnosis or participating in an ASD program, ask them supportively why and respond to their questions and concerns. Also remind your child that, even if they share the diagnosis with the school, they will take the same classes as other students, live in the same housing and participate in the same school activities. The support staff are located in a separate area and will not be involved in any of their classes or day-to-day activities.

You may also want to ask your child's counselor for help, or look at the website of the colleges your child is considering, for information that might address your child's concerns.

The bottom line: as outstanding as your child is, he or she will need support at college—so encourage, cajole, and enlist the help of others to make sure he or she asks for it.

The Friends Program

My awareness of the issues affecting college students on the Spectrum comes from decades of working with ASD kids and their parents. Back in 1993 I was asked to look into the large number of young children who were being asked to leave their preschool or private school setting because they didn't "fit."

I started The Friends Program, a therapeutic program that was different from existing programs in that it took a systems approach. We insisted that a parent participate in a parents' group that took place at the same time as the children's group, since preliminary studies demonstrated that the most improvement came when the parents really understood their child's issues. The other requirement was that the children had to be diagnosed before entering the program.

I have stayed in touch with many of these students, as their parents often contacted me with questions about how to best handle issues such as bullying, selecting a new school, and qualifying for services. They also shared life events such as high school graduations, college acceptances, first jobs, marriages, and children. I began notice that, once in college, many students experienced an increase in their symptoms. They simply were not prepared for the additional demands of college without the daily support of their parents.

These children and their parents inspired me to write this book. You will read their stories and reflections throughout the book. I trust you'll find their insights helpful, as I have.

NOTE

To protect their confidentiality the names of kids and parents have been changed and the names of the colleges removed.

But enough of the basics. Let's now look at the practical challenges these students will face at college.

KEY POINTS

» Many teens and their parents often have difficulty accepting the diagnosis of ASD because they believe that it does not differentiate them enough from students with more severe issues.

» Many of today's college students choose not to share their diagnosis or apply for disability services for fear of being seen as different by their friends.

» Students on the Spectrum need to understand and accept their diagnosis to secure academic, social, and mental health support at college.

How you can help

• Assess the current support services your child receives from family, school or outside professionals. Discuss these with your child and talk about how their needs can be met while they are at college. Realize that you, as a parent, can't step in to help with many of these needs.

• Remind your child that, even if they share their diagnosis with the school, they will be in the same classes as the other students, live in the same housing, and take part in the same school activities.

Chapter 2

The Transition to College —How Parents Can Help

When your child goes to college, your role changes because you cannot manage your child's day-to-day life any more. However, you can support your college adult academically, socially, and psychologically.

This chapter will look at ways you can help your child make the most of the college experience. Specifically, we'll look at:

- recognizing your new role

- developing strong communications

- fostering your child's independence before college

- accepting that your goals are not necessarily your child's goals

- selecting the "right" college

- applying for disability services

- supporting your child at college.

Recognizing your new role

As stated earlier, when a child turns 18, he or she is legally an adult. At that point most rights and responsibilities of the parent are transferred to the child, including the ability to get information on grades and healthcare issues, the responsibility to request support services, and the responsibility to sign legal documents.

As a parent you will still worry about your child but will not be able to monitor what they are doing or how they are feeling. You will not know how your child spends their days. You will not see whether they've done their homework or are bingeing on TV, playing video games or watching YouTube.

This change can be especially challenging when your child is on the Spectrum and you have managed their life up to this point. Moreover, ASD children are more challenged by transitions than many of their peers. So, the college transition will be more difficult for you and your child than it will be for most neurotypical families.

If you had a close relationship with your child up to this time, there is a good chance that will continue in college. They may still seek your advice, but you must accept that you cannot handle all their issues for them. And they will probably rely on you less and less as they become more independent, confident, and involved in school activities.

Setting boundaries for you and your child can help. One mother described how she and her husband did this: "I can still see Steve crying, 'I can't do any better,' and I said, 'Yes, you can. I've seen your work. You can do this. Go back to your room.' Then he would come back an hour or so later with a work of art. We talk about that now, and he says he still does that. First he has a meltdown. Then he does good work.

Later, during the first month of college, we let him come home every weekend. However, we decided that he was leaning on us too much, and we needed to *empower* him. So we told him we were busy the next weekend and that he had to study, so he wouldn't be able to come home. It was one of the hardest decisions we made regarding his college. It didn't go over great but we made it clear that we loved him, that he was fine, and that he could turn to his RA (Resident Advisor) if he needed help and support."

Over time, Steve realized that he could do things by himself. He internalized what his mother had been telling him. "He had always thought he could not do a paper. However, when he took a deep breath and gave himself a break, he was always able to go back, see the problems and come up with a solution. Even though he was upset at first, he realized that he did have good ideas and could transform them into a good paper." Karen, Steve's mother

Developing strong communications

How you and your child cope with the transition to college will depend, to a great extent, on how open your communication has been with your child. Developing a good rapport with your child before college is one of the most important ways you can support him or her at college.

Typically, the more often your family talks together, the more open the door will be for difficult topics. If conversations only arise when there is a problem, it is natural for your child to try to avoid talking or become defensive when conversations do occur. Set up time for regular conversation; for instance nightly dinners together with no phones allowed, evening strolls, or even family game nights.

Be as open-minded and encouraging as possible during these conversations. How do you think you would react hearing that your daughter is struggling with her math class? That she feels ignored by her "best" friend? That she is sexually active (or wants to be)? Remember, children, and especially teens, will be reluctant to be honest if they feel your response will be critical. I know several teens who do not share information with their parents because they think the parents do not listen to them or empathize with them.

Research shows that the more disconnected teens are from their parents, the more they turn to their peers or online sites for advice, support, and exploration. Research also shows that parents need to turn off their phones and computers at home or at mealtimes if they expect their children to do the same (van den Eijnden *et al.* 2010).

Good communication at home will make it easier for you to support your child. They will be more open about the challenges they encounter at college and will be more likely to ask for your input. Also, a strong rapport makes it less likely that your children will isolate themselves when problems occur. However, it's important that, once your child is in college, you pull back, respect and support boundaries, and encourage them to socialize with their new peers and to talk with their professors, teaching assistants (TAs), counselor or therapist for support.

Most college orientations emphasize the importance of not being a "helicopter parent." It is important to support your child while at the same time encouraging their autonomy.

Nothing is wrong with your child calling or texting you once a day at first. However, you shouldn't talk or text several times a day once they get settled into school. Talking with you several times a day will not give them much time to interact with friends, roommates, and classmates. Speaking with them weekly, preferably at a set day and time, is ideal. More frequent calls from your child may indicate a need for more support at school.

Don't take it personally if they forget to call you. Remember, organization is not their strength. Text them and let them know you missed talking with them. Ask if there is another time you could talk. You can gently suggest that they set a reminder by telling them that you are setting one on your phone.

One mother I talked with stressed that homesickness is a big issue with students whose parents have been a pillar of support their entire lives. She recommended visiting during parents' weekend, sending gift boxes of their favorite baked goods, and texting about what is going on at home, while staying away from telling them how to live their lives. When you send a funny text, the children are more likely to text about something going on with them. When the conversation turns to telling them what to do, the communication may come to an abrupt end.

Another parent decided she was too involved in her son's life and came up with a way to stay in touch without being overly involved.

> "The hardest part was pushing them out of the nest, moving the nest a little higher, pushing them out again and moving the nest a little higher," said Karen, who devised a simple way to keep in touch informally, through food. "His college was fairly close by. He was in a dorm, and I know what boys are like. I would pick up 30 hamburgers and French fries, meet him and say, 'Hey, I was in the area. Why don't you bring these to your dorm guys?' Steve's response was typically, 'That's awesome.' I felt connected without involving myself in his life." Karen, Steve and Sarah's mother

Perhaps the most important point about communicating with your child is that he or she needs to hear over and over how much you love them, that you know how hard they work, and that you truly believe in them.

How you can develop strong communication with your child

- Make dinner a phone-free time. No phone call or text is that urgent. Remember: if you cannot go without your phone you cannot expect your child to do so.

- If you cannot have dinner with your children, you cannot expect them to stop what they are doing to chat with you when you ask.

- Share with your child things that were interesting or frustrating about your day, and describe how you coped. Ask the same of them. They can learn that nobody has a perfect day.

- Check which videos or TV shows they enjoy. Watch some with them. Be careful not to be too critical.

- If your child has stopped talking with you, ask what is going on. They may be angry, afraid of how you will respond to something that is troubling them, or may have turned to peers or the Internet for support.

Fostering your child's independence before college

To ease the transition to college—for both you and your child—you should encourage your child to be more independent while in high school. You can start by encouraging your child to take responsibility for many day-to-day activities such as getting themselves up, getting to school, and doing their schoolwork without reminders. Show them how to make simple meals, do their own laundry, and manage their money.

It is also important you teach your child to become their own advocate in high school. They must find out who to talk to if they are upset about a class or a teacher and, if they do not feel that that person heard them, how to engage a different advisor. Remind them that you are there for support and to brainstorm solutions to problems, but they need to take the lead.

This is also a time for your child to begin self-regulating behaviors that could become a problem if left unchecked. For instance, if your child spends hours watching YouTube, playing video games, or pursuing a narrow area of interest, they need to moderate that behavior. If they are addicted to any behavior, help wean them from those activities. If that is not successful, have them see a mental health professional who has expertise in that behavior. This is important because students who don't regulate these behaviors before college may miss assignments, get poor grades, and become depressed and anxious (Steiner-Adair and Barker 2013).

Another great way to foster your child's independence and confidence is to enroll them in a summer school class at a local university or a university-sponsored summer program for high school students. Residential summer programs on campus enable students to experience dorm life; have roommates; get to meals, courses, and activities on their own; wash their clothes and do their homework, all without parental support.

In summary

- Encourage your child to manage day-to-day activities. (Chapter 3 goes into more detail on this topic.)

- Ask your child what he or she would do if upset at school, so that they can get used to the idea of advocating for themselves.

- Consider enrolling your child in a residential summer program so they get used to being away from you and managing day-to-day life.

Accepting that your goals are not necessarily your child's goals

All parents have dreams for their kids, but it is important you recognize that your goals and dreams may not match what your child wants. Children begin to absorb their parents' expectations in elementary school. By the time they are in high school and college, far too many students suffer from anxiety and depression, which is often rooted in trying to meet what they believe to be their parents' expectations.

When you consciously or unconsciously suggest that your child must excel academically, be accepted at a top school, or pursue a particular career, you are unnecessarily contributing to your child's stress. This added stress isn't good for any student, let alone one who is already managing ASD. In fact, this anxiety is a major contributing factor when students opt out of the college path altogether, believing that they will never meet their parents' expectations.

Parents need to acknowledge their child's academic and career interests, and understand that physical wellbeing, connections with peers, and time with friends and family are important, and perhaps more important to their long-term success than academic achievements or career choice.

So, set your goals aside and ask your child about his or her goals. Here are some questions to get you started.

- How does your child feel about going to college?

- What do they want to do professionally (understanding that this may change over time)?

- If they're interested in college, what do they want to study?

- What type of college environment do they want? Do they want to be a big fish in a small pond, or a small fish in a larger pond? How about competitiveness—does that bother them?

- How comfortable are they with living on the other side of the country? In what region of the country would they like to go to school? Is this where they see themselves living after college?

- What types of extracurricular activities—clubs, sports, etc.—interest them?

Alternatives to college

One important consideration is that your child may not want to go away to college right away, or at all. How would you know? Is your child enthusiastically completing the college applications, or is it a daily battle? If your child starts skipping classes, not working on the applications, and not asking teachers for recommendations, they may be trying to tell you they are either not interested or not yet ready for college.

If your child is procrastinating, have a relaxed discussion about what might be getting in the way. Reassure them that if they do not want to go to the colleges you or their counselor suggest (or if they don't want to go to college at all), you are open to other possibilities. This may also be a good time for them to see a therapist or psychiatrist to make sure an underlying issue such as depression or anxiety isn't at play.

For your part, you could see if the school counselor has any insight into what is happening. You may want to consult with a counselor specializing in college admissions.

A counselor who has experience with students on the Spectrum would be ideal. Talking with other people with whom your child confides—a grandparent, coach, or teacher mentor—may give you some insights.

It could also be a good time to explore alternatives such as having your child get a job, do volunteer work, or attend a community college for a year or two. Most of these colleges feed into state universities.

Some students, especially those who feel overwhelmed by the daily grind of high school or are otherwise anxious about attending college, could benefit from a gap year. A year off before attending college can give them a chance to clear their mind of the stress from high school or to explore a passion. They may want to live in another country, work on a political campaign, explore an artistic passion, do research, or work with children. For some, the gap year provides an opportunity to practice living away from home. This works especially well if they feel supported by their parents and are in a structured program such as an internship in organic farming, volunteering at a theater, a community service project in after-school programs, or working on a political campaign.

If your child takes a gap year, they may want to start by first being accepted by a college, then asking the college to defer for a year. The nice thing about this scenario is they do not have to end their gap year with the stress of applying for college.

Sarah and her mother were not sure if college was the best choice for her after graduation. Her mother said: "As the time for applying to school and moving away from home approached, Sarah's anxiety increased. She stayed home for a year, got a paid job and studied her passion, dance. But during that gap year an opportunity arose that she would have never thought of before."

Sarah explained: "For some reason, two weeks before college, my mom and I felt that I wasn't supposed to do it and instead I studied dance for a year. I was planning on going to college after that. But during that year off I applied to a non-profit dance company and was accepted. So, I decided to defer college another year. They specifically asked me to come back so I'm going to do so as long as they want me. I'll go to college afterwards. This experience taught me that I can manage life on my own. If you would have told me two years ago that I'd be living in another city on my own, I would not have believed you." Sarah and Karen, Sarah's mother

A change of plans

It's also important to realize that your child's goals may change. I know students who found college overwhelming. After the first quarter or semester exams they told their parents they did not want to return to school. In other cases, the schools told the students to take a leave of absence because they had not completed any of their required work and had not responded when teachers and clinicians offered support.

For some of these students, the social world was too stressful. Others "coped" by escaping to computer games and watching videos. In some cases, the students had even considered suicide.

Some of these students were on the Spectrum but not diagnosed until they were in college. Others had been diagnosed primarily with Attention Deficit Hyperactivity Disorder (ADHD) and were re-diagnosed with more complex issues when they crashed at college. All these children had received extensive support in high school. However, none of them took advantage of their colleges' support systems, especially in terms of seeing a mental health professional.

Some parents were shocked; others were angry; and still others were not surprised at their child's change of heart. In such situations it's important to recognize that the decision to leave school (or to act in a way that the school asks you to leave) may be a cry for help. College may just be too much, or it may no longer fit the child's goals and interests. It's important for parents to pause, find out more, and work with the child to develop an alternative plan. Dr. Hibbs and Dr. Rostain (2019) in their recent book, *The Stressed Years of Their Lives: Helping Your Kid Survive and Thrive During Their College Years*, talk about their experiences, as both parents and mental health professionals, when their children decided that college was not the right choice for them. They share the stress they underwent as parents, partners, and professionals who treat adolescents and college students who are experiencing anxiety and depression. The authors explore the importance of listening to their children's calls for help and their need for structure as they explore their individual education and career paths.

Some of these young adults are now seeing individual therapists or psychiatrists, and many families are in therapy together to deal with their teen's sense of being a failure.

There are alternative paths to success if college does not work out. For example, one of the students who had experienced suicidal ideation and left school after the first semester, now attends a community college, works at a hospital and is writing a book. Another student who decided that college was not for him also left after the first semester. He is now training to become a gourmet chef, and studying organic gardening and farming.

College is not the only path to success and is not necessarily the right path for all students. The challenge is that the parents stick together and support each other so that they can empower their young adult.

How you can support your child's goals

- Let your child know that you will love them no matter what they do. They need to know that it really is not important that they go to your alma mater or pursue the same career that you did.

- Take time to calmly discuss goals and college options with your child in a quiet, comfortable way.

- Ask questions but avoid "cross-examining" your child about their concerns or anxieties. If you have difficulty doing this, ask a therapist or counselor for help.

- The last year of high school will be less stressful if your child has already been accepted by a college. See if he or she is willing to reduce extracurricular activities to free up time to work on applications. Also, consider reducing the number of colleges your child applies for, or pursue an early-decision application. An early-decision application means that if you are accepted to the university or college to which you apply, then you must agree to enroll at that school. If they are not accepted, the applicant may be rejected or placed in the general application group.

  Early action plans are nonbinding—students receive an **early** response to their **application** but do not have to commit to the college until the normal reply date. Many students choose this option to see who provides the best financial aid package. A high school counselor or admissions counselor can help with this.

- If your child is interested in a gap year, look into programs. Again, a high school counselor or college admission counselor may have ideas.

Selecting the "right" college

Assuming that your child has determined that college is the right path, it is time to review colleges. In doing so, keep in mind that a school's ASD, mental health and disability services may be more important to your child's success than any academic program. More specifically, students and parents should consider factors such as:

- Do they offer programs specifically designed for ASD students?

- What is the typical wait time to get services?

- Are the school's mental health services available 24/7?

- What types of providers are on staff?

- Do the providers have expertise in working with students on the Spectrum or do they refer them to disability services for support?

- What is the ratio between students and providers?

- Are students able to register and make a first appointment online or must they go to the Student Health Services clinic? Many schools are making it easier to set up appointments online.

- Does the school welcome students coming with their parents for orientation or do they require the students to come alone?

- Is there a special time set aside during orientation where parents and their children can meet the university medical center and mental health staff and have their children give the staff permission to talk with the parent should an issue arise?

- Does the clinic encourage its therapists to contact their client's previous therapist, upon consent?

- What do other ASD students and their families say about the school?

Some other points for consideration
SIZE OF THE SCHOOL

Smaller colleges may be a better match for students who are overwhelmed by large groups of people, loud noises, and unpredictable social situations such as student protests. A smaller school typically offers smaller class sizes and provides less of a change from high school.

On the other hand, the wide array of classes and majors at large universities provides students with more choices and the chance to find a better fit with their areas of interest. The challenge is that freshmen are often required to attend large lectures in general areas before they can participate in smaller classes, which are better suited to the ASD students' social temperament and areas of interest.

Look into whether students are allowed to take some of the larger classes online, away from the loud noises, tight space, and rapid verbal exchanges. If the students can watch the lecture online, they may be able to attend the smaller study sessions led by the TAs, and see their professor during office hours.

HOUSING

Freshmen are often clustered in a common area of the campus. If your child is highly sensitive to noises, smells, and other sensory issues, find out if the school offers private rooms. (See Chapter 3 for more information about housing and roommates.)

Alternatively, if students go to school near their homes, they can live at home and take classes on the college campus. Doing so, however, will deprive them of the experience of living on their own, which may be as important as any academic program.

Fortunately, a growing number of colleges are posting specific information about the type of disability services that they offer for students with medical, academic, mental health, and ASD issues. The information typically describes the application process. This trend may be due to the increase in the number of suicides or threats of suicides on college campuses, as well as the number of lawsuits against universities because of how they handled various mental health crises. Whatever the rationale, the added information can make selecting the college a bit easier.

Ways to find out about a college's mental health services

- Make the school's ASD and mental health services a primary factor in evaluating potential colleges.

- Before applying, research the types of mental health providers on staff, their services, training, credentials, expertise, and availability for working with students on the Spectrum.

- When visiting campuses, stop by the student health clinic and inquire about their services.

Applying for disability services

Navigating the nuts and bolts of getting services is hard enough for parents, high school counselors, and college advisors, so it is easy to see how overwhelmed a student might feel in approaching this challenge. Here are some important things to understand:

- Students may not apply for disability services until they are accepted at the university. This means you and your child need not worry that the need for disability services could adversely impact his or her acceptance to a university. Legally, a student's mental health issues or other disabilities cannot be a consideration of acceptance into a college or university. Under the Americans with Disabilities Act (ADA), the admissions staff is not allowed to ask for, or accept, any information about a student's disability. Contrary to one popular myth, high school transcripts do not indicate whether or not students have disabilities (Hamblet 2014).

- College services do not work the same way as high school services do. Colleges are under no obligation to locate students with disabilities and give them the same accommodations they received in high school (Hamblet 2014).

- An IEP or 504 plan from high school does not automatically guarantee special services in college. An IEP can help and should be supplemented by letters from your child's high school IEP team, current therapist, and/or psychiatrist.

- In college, students with learning differences, disabilities, or mental health diagnoses have to meet the same academic requirements as their neurotypical classmates. They must take the same required courses, keep the required grade point averages, and score as well on standardized tests as any other student. Many high school students who went to small schools and/or received a lot of support, may find meeting the academic and organizational demands of college difficult. That difficulty can exacerbate their mental health issues.

- Colleges do not fall under the Individuals with Disabilities Education Act (IDEA), which is why IEPs are not extended past high school. Colleges do have to follow federal and civil rights laws, including Section 504 of the Rehabilitation Act of 1973 and the ADA. The goal of these laws is to ensure equal access for people with disabilities and to protect them from discrimination. The extent and quality of mental health and disability services varies greatly from college to college. Many colleges find it hard to provide services because of the high demand for, compared to the limited number of, qualified clinicians. It is not unusual to find that a top university does not provide services other than extended test time because of a lack of funding for disability services.

The process

If the school doesn't have a discrete ASD program, ASD students who are seeking services need to apply for them. Most schools require that the student fill out forms (probably online) at the start of the school year, meet with the staff at the campus health center and/or the disability program, and submit their documentation.

Students are responsible for applying for accommodations and services on time. So, it is important that your child be emotionally and mentally able to independently apply for services. If not, it is unlikely he or she will seek, get, or utilize the services needed to succeed in college.

This goes back to the fact that parents must prepare their children for college by giving them more responsibility for arranging, scheduling, and following through on mental health interventions and other responsibilities in high school.

The evaluation

The college's mental health staff will conduct an initial evaluation if the student has never been evaluated. The student may need to go to an outside professional if the school's mental health services department does not have enough staff to do the evaluation in a timely manner.

The college might not consider the student eligible for special services, even though their high school did. If students are denied services, they have the right to express a grievance based on the ADA/Section 504 Grievance Procedure regarding the school's allocation of services. This procedure provides a process to address student concerns of potential disability-based discrimination, or the denial of access to isability-related accommodations or services. These forms should be available in the college's disability office.

It may take one to two months before your child learns if he or she has qualified for disability services. However, they could be seen in less than a month if they feel that their mental health issues will impact their daily functioning and potentially result in serious depression or anxiety.

If your child qualifies for disability services, typically a letter outlining the types of accommodations required is distributed to the teachers. The letter should also have the name and contact information of the disability services professional they should contact if they have any questions.

Although students may have a specific person to contact in the disabilities program, that person typically does not ensure everything is running smoothly (Hamblet 2011). The onus is on the student to report to the disability services manager if a teacher does not comply with the plan.

Colleges have leeway in the types of accommodations they make (e.g., allowing a substitute course in place of a requirement). Obviously, this is an issue if the class is required for graduation. Students need to check graduation requirements carefully when they research schools. They should not assume that they will receive a substitution even if their high school provided them (Hamblet 2014).

How you can encourage your child to apply for disability services

- Remind your child that ultimately it will be up to them to get the type of support they think would help. Discuss the issue ahead of time so that they understand that, because they are legally adults, they will have to give consent for all types of medical and mental health services because of the Healthcare Insurance Portability and Accountability Act of 1996 (HIPAA).

- Encourage your child to apply for disability services and to set up an intake with a mental health professional even before they learn if they have qualified for services.

- Ask your child's therapist to talk with your child about the importance of continued support at college.

- Emphasize that seeing a therapist or utilizing disability services is smart. It will not label them as different. In fact, most students need some type of support and everyone is different in one way or another.

- Make sure your child understands that he or she is not alone. More and more students entering college today have been diagnosed with a mental health disorder or are diagnosed during the first year at college. As noted earlier, many college students would be surprised by how many other students at their school receive mental health services.

- Help your child see that getting services is a private process; it is not shared with other students.

- Ask your child to give permission for the staff to contact you if they have any concerns. The mental health professionals cannot disclose what they talk about with your child without specific consent. Ask your child to give the education support center this same type of permission.

- Remind your child that if they do not qualify for services there are other paths for support. For example, they could see a school or private therapist who has expertise in working with students on the Spectrum, or go to the campus resource centers that help students with academics, organization, and planning, such as the Schwab Foundation centers.

- Review Chapter 1 for tips on how to talk to your child about accepting their diagnosis and getting support services.

- Read *Successful Transitions to College for Students with Disabilities* by Elizabeth C. Hamblet (n.d.) for a good overview of the application process.

Supporting your child at college

As a parent of an ASD college student, it's understandable that you will be concerned about how your child is managing the ASD symptoms. Unfortunately, monitoring your child at college is complicated because colleges are bound by various privacy laws. Specifically, colleges are required to follow federal laws including the HIPAA, which forbids colleges from speaking with parents without their child's consent.

Specifically, HIPAA restricts the college from revealing information that relates to:

- the student's past, present, or future physical or mental health, or condition

- the provision of healthcare to the student

- the past, present, or future payment for the provision of healthcare to the student.

By definition, this restricts your access to information about your child's treatment unless your child formally gives the college permission to tell you about his or her mental health or wellbeing. So, once your child is at college, the school will typically ask the student's consent to contact you if they are concerned about the student's academic performance or physical or mental health. It is important that your child, during the intake process for the mental health clinic and disability services, gives the clinician that permission. This topic is also covered in Chapter 6, Mental Health Services in Today's Colleges.

Getting information about academic performance is different. That is covered by the Family Educational Rights and Privacy Act (FERPA), a federal privacy act that gives parents certain rights and protections with regards to their children's educational records. FERPA provides ways that a school may (but is not required to) share information from an eligible student's academic record without the student's consent. Under FERPA rules, schools may:

- disclose academic records to parents if the student is claimed as a dependent for tax purposes, or if the child has had a health or safety emergency in the past

- inform parents if a student, under the age of 21, has violated any law or policy concerning the use of alcohol or controlled substances.

Additionally, a school official may share information that is based on classroom or dorm behavior. For more information, go to *Parents' Guide to the Family Educational Rights and Privacy Act: Rights Regarding Children's Educational Records* (FERPA).[1]

Some schools, like Tufts University, take a more proactive approach by prompting students to provide this permission to parents. Before the child even goes to the school, Tufts sends a letter to the parents explaining that the child will receive a consent form asking their permission to contact the parents if there are significant health, mental health or academic performance issues. This type of preventive approach gives parents a chance to discuss these issues with their child before a serious problem occurs.

While the consent-to-contact helps, most schools do not have this process in place and the chances are that you will not hear anything from the administration until your child displays serious medical or mental health issues or is in danger of failing a class.

When a student attends a program designed for students on the Spectrum, they often have an advisor who helps them organize their day, keeps track of their grades, and helps them get academic help and mental health support as needed. This is another important reason to consider one of the growing numbers of colleges with programs for ASD students. Two such programs—Marshall University's College Program for Students with Autism Spectrum Disorders and Pace University's OASIS Program—are described in Chapter 6, Mental Health Services in Today's Colleges.

---

1   www2.ed.gov/ferpa

Staying connected while respecting their autonomy

- Set a day and time when you will call, even if the schedule may change.

- Write down the things that concern you. Don't flood your child with questions but see what comes up in conversation and address only the most important issue.

- Figure out the best way to connect with your child. For many students it is asking about their favorite part of the day.

- Send funny cartoons when you see them.

- Connect with a friend who also has a child in college. It is a way to "normalize" some of your concerns.

- If your child is seeing a therapist, have a Skype talk with them if they have consent.

KEY POINTS

Recognizing that your goals are not necessarily your child's goals

» It's important to take time to understand your child's goals. Remember, their goals are not necessarily your goals.

» Speaking with other people with whom your child confides—a grandparent, coach or teacher mentor—may give you insight into your child's concerns about college.

» A year off may be a perfect solution for a student who feels stressed and exhausted.

» If your child wants to take a gap year, it may be easier if they apply to college before their break so that they do not have to worry about it during the break.

Applying for disability services

» The school's mental health services may be more important for your child's success than its academic rankings or offerings.

» Colleges are required to provide some mental health and disability services. However, the quality, quantity, and availability of those services vary dramatically between institutions.

» Students may not apply for disability services until they are accepted into the university. College and university cannot consider the student's mental health issues or other disabilities when evaluating an application.

» Most colleges require that students with physical, medical, learning and neurodevelopmental disorders apply for disabilities services to get accommodations such as extended time for exams, a reduced course load or academic support.

» An IEP or a 504 plan in high school does not guarantee disability services in college.

» If the mental health issues do not appear until college, a student can still apply for services, but typically he or she will need to be evaluated first.

» All students are required to meet the school's academic standards.

» The more a school knows about a student's diagnoses, the better they will be able to help that student. The student, not the parent, needs to share this information with the school.

» It may take one to two months before they hear back if they qualify for disability services. However, they could be seen in less than a month if they feel that their mental health issues will impact their daily functioning and potentially result in serious depression or anxiety.

» Some colleges, such as Marshall University and Pace University, offer special programs for students with ASD.

Supporting your child at college

» Your role and rights as a parent change dramatically once your child goes to college.

» Developing a habit of regular and open communications with your child is crucial if you hope to have a strong relationship with your child during college.

» Your child needs to know that you want to hear how they feel, and that you will find a way to help them feel less pressured.

» Make sure your child knows that you care more about their health and wellbeing than about their grades.

» In college, a student's social world and community involvement are as important as their grades.

Recap of how you can help
How you can develop strong communication with your child

- Make dinner a phone-free time. No phone call or text demands an immediate response.

- Start a dinner conversation about things that were interesting or frustrating about your day, and describe how you coped. Ask the same of all family members.

- Ask which YouTube videos, TV shows and Internet websites they enjoy and watch a few with them. Be careful not to be critical.

- If your child has stopped talking with you, ask what is going on and assure them that you are always interested in them. Always try to be non-judgmental.

How you can foster your child's independence

- Encourage your child to manage day-to-day activities. (Chapter 3 goes into more detail on this topic.)

- Ask your child what they would do if something upset them at school, and encourage self-advocacy.

- Research residential summer programs that might interest your child and give them experience living with roommates away from home, adapting to a new schedule and program of activities.

How you can support your child's goals

- Let your child know that you will love and support them no matter their choice of school or field of study, if that is how you feel.

- Discuss goals and college options with your child in a calm, non-pressured way.

- Ask questions but avoid "cross-examining" your child about their concerns or anxieties. Consider seeking help from a therapist or counselor if your child is not responsive.

- Explore if your child is willing to reduce extracurricular activities to free up time for applications.

- If your child is interested in a gap year, look into programs together. A college admission counselor may have suggestions.

How you can help select the "right" college

- Make the school's ASD and mental health services a primary factor in evaluating potential colleges including the types of providers, services offered, and their availability.

- When visiting campuses, stop by the student health clinic and inquire about their services.

- Remind your child that, as adults, it will be up to them to get the type of support they need.

- Help your child see that getting services is a private process; it is not shared with other students.

- Explore alternative support services if your child does not qualify for institutional help.

- Review Chapter 1 for tips on how to talk to your child about accepting their diagnosis and getting support services.

- Read *Successful Transitions to College for Students with Disabilities* by Elizabeth C. Hamblet for a good overview of the application process.

How you can support your child at college

These points, mentioned earlier with respect to staying connected to your child, are equally important in the context of supporting them at school:

- Plan ahead a day and time when you will call.

- Write down the things that concern you. Don't flood your child with questions but see what comes up in conversation, follow their lead as much as possible, and address only the most important issues.

- Send funny cartoons or articles that you can talk about.

- Connect with a friend who also has a child with special needs in college. It is a way to "normalize" some of your concerns, and develop a support system.

— Chapter 3 —

College Freshman Basics

Congratulations, your child's going to college! Now what?

Going to college is a big step for anyone. And it is a bigger step for students on the Spectrum who struggle, more than their peers, with the practical challenges of day-to-day.

In this chapter, we examine the practical skills that all students need to thrive at college, and why these skills are particularly important for students on the Spectrum. Specifically, we will cover:

- time management and study skills

- housing: a shared space

- money management

- self-care

- meals

- medications and medical records.

Most college students are on their own for the first time, responsible for managing their time, their money, and themselves. These challenges are all the more daunting for students on the Spectrum. As more and more of these high-functioning teenagers attend college, they face multiple challenges, which many of their classmates do not face and often do not understand.

The situation is further complicated by the fact that many teenagers with ASD also suffer from other disorders that can disrupt their organizational and planning skills, such as ADHD, anxiety, or depression. We talk more about "comorbidity" challenges in Chapter 5.

Zoe is a 21-year-old who attends a well-known liberal arts school on the East Coast. She gets good grades but is well aware that it takes her longer to do everything compared to her peers, such as getting up in the morning, making the transitions between classes, and doing her schoolwork.

She struggles with daily life skills, time management, and study skills. She is often depressed and anxious, which adversely affects her physical health. This undermines her ability to get her work done on time, which, in turn, makes her even more anxious and depressed.

For Zoe, managing her daily living is much more challenging than dealing with social communication and relationships, issues that may be more challenging for many other students on the Autism Spectrum (Child Mind Institute 2016).

Time management and study skills

One of the biggest challenges for college students is time management. In one study, several students reported academic success but feeling overwhelmed in the organizational demands of their daily lives and homework (Gelbar, Shefcyk, and Riechow 2015).

It's understandable. In pre-college days, parents often manage their child's day. The parents wake their kids up, prepare breakfast, and drive them to school to ensure they are on time. Parents often remind their kids of pending tasks, check homework, and make sure the child takes any prescribed medication.

Parents of ASD children typically go several steps further by, for example, teaming up with school advisors and counselors to help their child manage schedules, organize daily living tasks and meet responsibilities. This support allows these students to be successful enough to be accepted into college, although they probably are not fully prepared for their time there.

Once the children go to college, the parents are no longer there to help. The students assume responsibility for their day-to-day lives. Unfortunately, this can be the downfall for many students, including some intellectually gifted ones. Far too many students leave college of their own accord, or are asked to leave, even though they are capable of doing the work. They leave because they lack the management and study skills to meet their academic responsibilities.

> For some students, procrastination is the problem. As Steve, one of the students who was interviewed for this book, said: "The hardest thing was totally managing my time. I'd put off starting projects or studying until the last few days, and then I'd be shocked when I got a worse grade than I had expected."

Online distractions are a problem for some students who endlessly play games online or watch YouTube, leaving them too tired to do their work or get to classes. These online distractions are often the reason students fail to complete assignments, resulting in poor grades (Ehmke 2019).

Other students, including those on the Spectrum, might be conscientious but still struggle. Unfortunately, many are reluctant to ask for academic assistance. Most of the students interviewed for this book knew they had benefited from academic help in high school. However, most didn't seek these services in college, even after strong encouragement from their parents, because they thought that they did not need help or just wanted to appear "normal." Their resistance to accepting help was a tremendous roadblock in getting the academic, social, and mental health support they needed.

As Thomas, one of the students interviewed for this book, said: "I thought about study aids but I didn't really avail myself of them as much as I thought I would. They offered me a note-taker, but I decided ultimately against it. They offered me time-and-a-half on tests but I only used that for two classes where I had a lot of handwritten tests. I didn't use it for most things."

Sometimes the problem is that the student just under-estimates the amount of work the classes will be. As the mother of one student explained: "Part of the problem was that he signed up for too many demanding courses. He took several technical math and science classes because he thought he had to get all of them done his freshman year. He ended up getting so overwhelmed that he froze. He would not respond to a teacher who was concerned about him not coming to class, turning in his work or responding to his phone calls." Joan, Gabe's mother

Plagiarism and cheating

An unfortunate side effect of poor time management is cheating, including plagiarism, which students may revert to when they have not completed assignments or studied for a test. This type of activity occurs even at elite universities.

Cheating includes copying a friend's answers to a test or receiving a copy of a test beforehand. This is a major reason why tests are often given in different versions. Students caught cheating or helping another cheat (such as by taking a picture of a test and sending it to a friend) may be expelled.

Plagiarism is usually the result of copying a section of a published paper without giving the author credit. Teachers are highly attuned to detecting this type of behavior. Most schools now have computer programs that can detect if a section of a paper was copied from another publication without giving the author credit. These systems can also pick up if the paper was copied from a website that provides papers on a wide range of topics. This is one reason why many students must submit their work in a digital format. Of course, it is all right to use quotes from a book or paper, but there are limits on how much material can be used and the author must always be given credit and cited properly.

How you can help your child manage time more effectively

- Give your child increasing responsibilities for daily activities, such as getting themselves out of bed and ready for the day ahead.

- Explain to your child how important it is that he or she gets the course outline for the quarter or semester (which may be available online). The outline may include important information like due dates for projects, test dates, and lab hours.

- Show your child how to transfer the information from the course outline to a planner or phone. Encourage them to do that for all the classes.

- Explain how a mobile phone can help your child stay up-to-date with school and activity schedules. For example, encourage your child to use a smart phone to:

- list daily class schedules on the calendar and set alarms

- post the dates for quizzes, tests, and other due dates

- schedule reminders a week or two before tests or other important due dates

- schedule another reminder the day before those milestones, and a final reminder on that day.

• Discuss the possibility of getting a "buddy" to study with.

• Discuss cheating and plagiarism with your child, and explain the ramifications of being found guilty of either of these unethical behaviors.

• If your child received help with homework and assignments in high school, encourage them to contact the disability services office before the semester begins (if possible) or on the first day of school. After they apply for disability services they will be informed if they qualify and which services are available to them.

• Contact the school if you are concerned about your child's academic progress. (See Chapter 2 for more information about this topic.)

Steve, a participant in The Friends Program, initially did a great job organizing his day including going to his classes, completing his homework, and socializing. However, his increased social activity, a new girlfriend, and his anxiety about homework impacted his experiences with time-management issues at college: "If anything, I probably would have tried to work on homework earlier because that way I got things done way before the deadlines. That was a real blessing. Everyone else was stressing out, but I didn't worry about it. Unfortunately, I did not work that way the rest of my time at college." He also explained how he learned time-management skills: "I just taught myself. I probably should have sought more help. I talked to mom and sometimes to my teachers."

Housing: a shared space

Before students move in, most schools ask them about their areas of interest, lifestyle preferences (e.g., night owl or early riser, noise levels, and study habits), and other information to match students with classmates who share similar interests and lifestyles.

There are generally lots of types of dorms. There will probably be male, female, and co-ed dorms, and possibly dorms for transsexual, gay, or lesbian students. Some floors will be quieter and others will welcome evening gatherings and parties.

It is not uncommon for students with ASD to request private rooms due to sensory-regulatory issues, anxiety, and sleep difficulties. It is helpful to have a therapist write a letter supporting such a request. The upside of having a private room is that the students may be more relaxed and sleep better. The downside is that this choice may limit their social opportunities, making it more difficult to meet their fellow classmates.

Even when roommates are friends, issues can arise because they are living in a shared space. Potential differences include housekeeping, music, and sleep patterns. If the roommates work out their differences at the beginning, they may still be good friends.

Housekeeping is a major area of potential conflict. For some, dirty clothes go on the floor or over a chair until they run out of space. If keeping things orderly is important to your child, he or she should indicate that on the housing intake form.

It is important to accept roommates will have some annoying habits, but any potential conflicts should be talked about early on before they become issues. For instance, if your roommate snores it's better to get earplugs than to complain about something they probably can't change. But if a roommate leaves the room a total mess, it's good to discuss the matter and look for ways to fix the situation.

Another important issue to consider is sleep cycles. A growing number of studies have demonstrated how important sleep is for health and wellbeing. If a person likes to stay up late and the roommate likes to go to bed early, the two can find ways to accommodate each other. For example, the night owl can make sure the room is dark and quiet; or go somewhere else to study or socialize.

The early-to-bed students, in turn, will have to be quiet when getting up. Tools that helped the teenager sleep at home or at sleep-away nights (e.g., ear plugs, eye masks, or a white sound machine) may help at college, especially if the roommate keeps the lights on late, if the dorm floor is noisy, or if the blinds do not block the light well.

How you can help your child adjust to living with roommates

- Brainstorm solutions for how your child might suggest a compromise with the roommate if there is a disagreement. Remember, your child needs to resolve the issue. Do not address the issue directly with the roommate or Resident Advisor (RA).

- Share funny stories about your own roommate experiences and how you worked out any issues. (Yes, spouses count.)

- Explain how it helps to share expenses for extra room items, such as a refrigerator, and to have food items for sharing and other food for just them. Suggest your child keep the special things they do not want to share in a separate plastic container.

- Remind your child that part of being a roommate is sharing. A roommate might eat some of the teenager's favorite foods. It should not be a reason to end a friendship. Your child can always get more food.

- Provide a large laundry basket so that the students can just throw their things in until it is full.

- Suggest making a list of rules, such as who is responsible for regular cleaning.

- Read the book *Parties, Dorms, and Social Norms: A Crash Course in Safe Living for Young Adults on the Autism Spectrum* (Meeks and Masterson 2016) and encourage your child to read it. The book talks about many of the social issues students encounter on the college campus and offers good ideas for handling them.

Money management

For many students, college is the first time that they manage their own money. It is a challenge for many adolescents to plan what they will buy and determine what they can afford, especially when they have been dependent on their parents for financial support.

Long before students go to school, parents should discuss managing money. Parents should start by giving them a clear budget to manage at least six months before they go to college. The parents and child should lay out what the parents will cover and what the child will be responsible for. The budget plan should include who will pay for tuition, books, food, health insurance, transportation, and other expenditures. What are their obligations, such as student work hours and grades, to maintain their parents' financial support?

Another consideration is whether your child will have his or her own bank account with a debit or credit card, which will require them to monitor the account online and understand the consequences of overdrawing it or of being late with a payment. Parents can open a joint account in the child's senior year in high school, which gives the child time to learn to manage it. The bank should be part of a national ATM network to make it easier to make withdrawals and deposits at ATMs at or near the school. If possible, opening the account where the parent banks will make it easier to transfer money into the child's account.

It's also wise to look over your child's account weekly in the beginning, and then review it together at least once a month during the freshman year. Many students need ongoing reminders to check their bank balance, instruction on how to use the ATM, and directions as to what to do if their card is lost or stolen.

An unfortunate but real part of managing money is learning to avoid scams. You need to make sure your child is aware that there are scams that specifically target college students. For instance, many freshmen receive letters or emails that look exactly like the welcoming letters they received from their new bank. The difference is that the letters ask for a Social Security number, password or birthday to "confirm the information." It is important that your child knows that any email that asks for confidential data (such as their name, Social Security number, credit card number or password) is a scam. Schools often have online videos and classes on this topic, but it is still vital that you discuss the topic with your child before the start of college.

How you can help your child manage money

- Consider setting up a joint bank account with your child before college, and teach him or her how to manage it and check the balance.

- Give your child a budget with responsibility for certain expenses the senior year of high school.

- Consider introducing your child to an app such as NerdWallet, which helps college students keep their budget balanced. Start such a program before they go to school.

- Alternative payment apps like Venmo are increasingly popular. Review with your child the scams associated with these before using them.

- Explain that your child should not open any additional credit card accounts, even though they often receive invitations in the mail.

- If it looks like managing money will be overwhelming for your child, check sites like Autism Speaks for helpful information on this topic.[1]

Self-care

Personal care—including taking care of daily personal hygiene, getting enough sleep, eating well, and taking medications—is critical to any student's success.

With the pressure of adjusting to college, personal care often slips through the cracks. It helps if students have a routine for sleep, meals, and hygiene before going to college. If the student is not comfortable showering with other people in the same bathroom, he or she will need to shower at a

---

1   www.autismspeaks.org

time when other students are gone. This anxiety may be even stronger for those students on the Spectrum who are super-sensitive to the sound of showers or toilets, or to fragrances and other odors, and who are self-conscious at the prospect of being seen bathing or dressing by other people.

To increase a feeling of privacy, it helps to have a plastic, waterproof shower caddy to hold shower and toiletry materials, so there is no need to go back into the dorm room for supplies.

College may be the first time many students do their own laundry. It is important to practice with your child at home so they learn, for example, the importance of separating whites from colors if they are going to use hot water.

Meals

Meals are an important time for students to socialize with others. Freshmen usually eat most meals in the cafeteria where the food may be different from what they had at home. For students on the Spectrum, the cafeteria may seem noisy and smelly. It helps if they have eaten in cafeterias at high school or camp, making them more familiar with those sights, sounds, and smells. If not, the student might want to eat during "off-hours."

Many students gain weight in their freshman year because they skip healthy meals. Then they become hungry as they stay up late to work or socialize, and order pizza or other high-calorie fast foods late at night. More and more campuses have late-night snacks shops where they can go to get healthy snacks like fruit smoothies, pitta bread and fresh vegetables with dip, tea, and fresh cookies to list a few. The goal is to help fight the trend of late-night pizzas and junk food. Many also have areas offering more nutritious snacks and after-breakfast snacks for those who sleep through the normal breakfast time. You need to stress how important good nutrition is for overall health and wellbeing.

Medications and medical records

If your child will be taking medication at college, they should bring an ID sheet with the name of their primary physician and/or psychiatrist; and the names, dose and frequency of their medications. If any of the pills are controlled substances, he or she needs to carry a copy of the prescription with the name and phone number of the prescribing physician. Also, make sure your child knows that they must file a police report if any of their controlled substances are lost or stolen. These rules apply to all students on medication.

Before your child goes to college, you need to determine whether they can manage their own medications. If not, students can arrange for a nurse at the student health center to manage the prescriptions. This is a good option for many students. However, it requires a visit the health center once or twice a day to pick up the medication.

If your child will be managing their own medications, they need instruction on how to do so safely. It is important that they discuss how to best manage their medication with their doctor or psychiatrist before they leave for college, including the risk of drinking alcohol or using other substances while they are on the medication.

A weekly or monthly pill box is helpful for organizing medications. Many psychiatrists recommend using a locked box for this purpose.

Alarms on phones are a great way to remind students when they need to take medications. It can be helpful to set two alarms; one reminder and another at the actual time to take the medication. The problem is that many of today's students do not look at their phones regularly enough to see the reminders or they ignore them, especially if the phone is set on vibration, and does not give them a visual or auditory reminder.

Finally, make sure your child understands that they should not share or sell the medications to fellow students, who may ask for them to help them study or to relieve stress. Giving friends drugs not prescribed for them could cause adverse and potentially life-threatening reactions, and is considered a felony in most states.

This process needs to start several months before college. The sooner your child starts managing medications, the more comfortable they will be with the process.

How you can help your child manage medications

- Have your child talk with their doctor or psychiatrist about any potential side effects of the medications.

- Help your child decide whether he or she should manage their medication, or have it administered by the school health office. If the latter, look into the health clinic and see if they dispense medications on a daily basis. Ask specifically about weekends and holidays.

- Train your child to manage his or her medication before going to college. Watch your child divide the medication and make sure that it is taken on a regular basis.

- Get a weekly pill container to hold medicines for one, two or three times a day, depending on what is needed. Buy an extra container in case they lose that one.

- Help your child set alarms on the mobile phone to manage their medication schedule.

KEY POINTS

» Virtually all students experience some stress and uncertainty while adjusting to college. These experiences are especially acute for students on the Spectrum.

» Many ASD students resist going to the services offered at their college because they think they do not need them or want to appear "normal."

» Time-management challenges include handling deadlines for projects and studying for tests. Mobile phones can help students stay on track and meet their deadlines.

» Independent-living challenges include handling money, eating properly, and getting enough sleep.

Recap of how you can help
How you can help your child manage time more effectively

- Give your child increasing responsibility for their daily activities.

- Explain the importance of having the course outline with important due dates for projects, test dates, and lab hours.

- Show your child how to transfer the information, for all the classes, from the course outline to a planner or smartphone.

- Discuss the possibility of getting a "buddy" to study with.

- If your child received help with homework and assignments in high school, encourage them to contact the disability services office before the semester begins (if possible) or on the first day of school.

- Contact the school if you are concerned about your child's academic progress. (See Chapter 2 for more information about this topic.)

How you can help your child adjust to living with roommates

- Brainstorm solutions for how your child might suggest a compromise with a roommate if there is a disagreement.

- Share funny stories about your own roommate experiences and how you worked out any issues.

- Explain how it helps to share expenses for extra room items such as a refrigerator, and suggest your child keep any special things they do not want to share in a separate container.

- Remind your child that part of being a roommate is **sharing**. It requires cooperation and flexibility.

- Encourage your child to look at books and articles about the social world of college. *Parties, Dorms, and Social Norms* (Meeks and Masterson 2016) is a good example.

How you can help your child manage money

As previously discussed, taking an active role in one's financial responsibility is a complex task for many college students. Some steps that may help with this challenge are:

- Consider setting up a joint bank account with your child before college, and teach him or her how to manage it and check the balance.

- Give your child a budget with responsibility for certain expenses in the senior year of high school.

- Consider introducing your child to an app such as NerdWallet, which helps college students keep their budget balanced. Start such a program before they go to school.

- Explain that your child should not open any additional credit card accounts and review some common ways that people are scammed.

- If it looks like managing money will be overwhelming for your child, check sites like Autism Speaks for helpful information on this topic. [2]

How you can help your child manage medications

- Have your child talk with their doctor or psychiatrist about any potential side effects of the medications.

- Help your child decide whether they should manage their medication, or have it administered by the school health office. If the latter, look into the health clinic and ask if they dispense medications on a daily basis, including weekends and holidays.

- Have your child manage their medication before going to college.

---

2   www.autismspeaks.org

- Get a weekly pill container to hold medicines for one, two or three times a day, depending on what is needed. Buy an extra case.

- Help your child set alarms on their mobile phone to manage their medication schedule.

Chapter 4

Emotional Challenges

For many college students, the academic and independent-living challenges are minor compared to the emotional issues they face, often for the first time. This can be especially true for students on the Spectrum.

This chapter will cover:

- stress, loneliness, anxiety and depression

- socializing and making friends

- bullying

- it's a matter of opinion: tolerating different perspectives

- self-advocacy

- risky behavior: drinking, drugs and sex

- the first six months.

Stress, loneliness, anxiety and depression

It's natural for students to feel stressed out at times, especially if they are at a residential college. After all, they have left their families, familiar surroundings and, perhaps, most of their friends. They may be anxious because of the financial burden the school places on their family, their own feelings of isolation, concerns about their academic performance, or a host of other issues.

All that is difficult enough. However, students with ASD experience loneliness, anxiety, and depression at rates higher than their non-ASD peers. In a recent survey, more than 75 percent of the ASD participants reported feeling left out, isolated, or lacking a friend "some of the time" or "most of the time" (Jackson *et al.* 2018). The findings from this survey are detailed in Chapter 5, Mental Health Issues.

A contributing factor to the sense of isolation and stress is that many students on the Spectrum have trouble reading social cues. Joan, Gabe's mother, explained how this was a problem for her son: "One of his biggest frustrations was having a crush on a girl who was not interested in him. He was unable to correctly interpret her social cues so he kept trying to get a date with her. Fortunately, one of her friends explicitly told him the girl was not interested in dating him."

Sarah's mother described a similar situation: "Sarah had a hard time talking on the phone. She has to take in the whole person. She needs multiple inputs to grab the whole conversation."

And Steve's mom said: "He wanted to invent a machine that you could put next to your head, almost like a cell phone, that would read your emotion and tell people what it was, because the message that he would often send wasn't always the message that people received. He thought that if he had this little machine that said 'angry' or 'scared' they would get the right message. And then he wanted one on the other person's heads so he would get the right message."

In one study, stress and depression were identified as key factors contributing to the students' resistance to getting the services that could help them (Mattila *et al.* 2010). These students were primarily studying engineering, technology and computer science, majors that many students think require less collaboration and group-focused projects than they actually do.

All this goes back to the importance of sharing the diagnosis with your child, and the need for your child to share the diagnosis with the student mental health center.

Managing stress

Many students "deal" with stress by watching YouTube videos, surfing online, or playing video games for hours. This is a poor way of coping when it takes the time they need for homework.

For ASD students who are overly sensitive to their environment, the problem is greater. Fortunately, many of these issues can be addressed at the onset by getting a private room, which eliminates all roommate issues. Students can seek disability accommodations, which would allow them to take tests in quiet rooms, attend classes online, and identify the sensory-sensitive locations on campus. Also, the ASD college student might eat in the cafeteria during the non-meal times to reduce sensory stimulation. Colleges with special programs for students on the Spectrum have integrated these issues into their services. Some of these programs are described in Chapter 6, Mental Health Services in Today's Colleges.

Stress-reducing activities are also important. Many students release stress through physical activity or special-interest groups such as running, swimming, team sports, singing, martial arts, or dance. The problem arises when these groups become competitive (as many do) and the goal of reducing stress vanishes. Instead, stress often increases as each game or performance approaches. For this reason, students on the Spectrum should consider non-competitive alternatives—pick-up games versus structured competitions, improvisation groups versus full theater productions.

Most schools have a wellness center that posts campus activities, coping strategies, and support groups online. Mental health centers also offer different services and resources for managing stress. See Chapter 6, Mental Health Services in Today's Colleges, for more details.

How you can help your child manage stress

- Share the activities that calm you down, such as taking five deep breaths, grasping your hands and stretching them to the back and then to the front, taking a walk, or listening to a favorite song or a meditation app.

- Help your child identify ways to reduce stress before there is a crisis. Have them think about options such as physical activities, games, artistic expression, meditation, yoga, or talking with a friend.

- Help your child manage interruptions. Make sure they know to turn off their phones and post a message on their door when they are not free to talk, chat, or respond to text messages.

- Encourage your child to give the school's academic and mental health staff permission to contact you if there is a concern.

- Help your child create a plan for obtaining emotional support through the school health office, a therapist, or support group.

Socializing and making friends

For many students on the Spectrum, the academic challenges pale compared to their challenges in understanding and engaging in social-emotional relationships with their classmates. (Roberts 2018). Meeks and Masterton (2016) provide an excellent guidebook on the social norms of college life for students on the Spectrum.

Recent research underscores the importance of the students' social capacity to relate to their peers, professors, and other administrative and support staff (White *et al.* 2019). Part of the problem is that many students on the Spectrum fear what their classmates might think if they knew about the ASD (and possibly other) diagnoses. In fact, most of the information collected by online studies about students' mental health identifies their fears of being rejected by their peers.

Likewise, many of the students I interviewed for this book wanted to make sure that I would not use their names or the name of their college. They had felt ostracized or bullied by classmates in high school, and feared that would happen again at college if they shared this personal information with their peers. The exceptions often are those students who came from families that had spoken openly about their medical and mental health issues since the time they were diagnosed.

Another reason for a lack of socializing is that typically children on the Spectrum only want to talk about their areas of interest, which may partially explain why they only want to meet people who share their interests. (It is true many people gravitate to those who share their interests or outlook. However, this tendency is much stronger for children on the Spectrum than for many of their peers.)

Obviously, this creates barriers to making new friends. This can also make college more challenging because the students will inevitably meet people with different styles and interests, starting (perhaps) with their roommates.

Indeed, roommates are often the first people college students meet on campus. Roommates who become friends can introduce each other to their friends, provide gentle reminders for time management, brainstorm solutions to problems and offer ideas for resources.

Ideally, roommates will be good friends, even if they have different interests.

Of course, it can be tricky to be friends with some people. Many college students are frustrated with roommates who, rather than engaging in small talk with them, checking in about their day or arranging to go to a meal or activity together, spend most of their awake time in the room on the computer, playing video games, gambling, or searching the Internet. If the relationship with their roommate is difficult, students can speak with their RA, who may be able to offer some insights or suggest a solution.

When a good friendship develops, it is important for students on the Spectrum to realize that being friends with a roommate does not necessarily mean they will be "best" friends and spend a lot of time together. They could easily have different majors, go to different classes, and have different interests.

Even if roommates don't socialize together, it's good for them to develop a rapport. Sometimes just asking the roommate about a favorite computer game, music, or class will bridge the gap and start a friendly relationship.

In general, it is best to have a wide range of friends. A student may enjoy having dinner with someone who likes to sit in the quiet section of the dining room, and then hang out with someone else who enjoys the same music or films.

It is also essential that the ASD student understands that conversation is a give-and-take process, otherwise classmates may stop responding to their comments because they are tired of hearing the ASD student talk about the same topic without showing interest in their views and activities.

One student developed insight about his condition from majoring in psychology. Rather than blurting out his thoughts or diagnoses as he did in high school, where he was bullied, he learned to share information when he felt it fit the class.

All the interviewed students have learned that they sometimes said too much and turned off peers. Some fortunate ones had a supportive adult who helped them see when and how sharing their diagnosis could be to their advantage. Most of the students I interviewed for this book who did not have that special mentor or therapist often felt as if their needs were overlooked or misunderstood on campus.

> As Gabe, another participant in The Friends Program, explained: "I had two roommates; one was really quiet. I probably didn't exchange more than 1,000 words with him, total, the entire year. Most of the time he was either studying or playing videogames. The other roommate was quiet too, but he was in the band. I tried out for the band, but did not make it. However, I became pretty close with this second roommate and met a lot of my friends through him."

How you can help your child socialize and make friends

- Describe how you made friends when you were in college, when starting a new job, or moving to a new city.

- While your child is in high school, encourage participation in clubs, teams and other social groups, so that they get used to interacting with others in different environments.

- Encourage your child to participate in a freshman orientation program as a way of meeting other college students. It is always nice to see a familiar face on campus.

- Encourage your child to consider support groups and special-interest groups that may help them interact better with fellow students.

- Also encourage your child to sign up for clubs that have activities that they enjoyed in high school or wanted to join. Most colleges have a wide range of student clubs, from music and hiking to current events and writing groups. These groups are a great way to meet people with shared interests.

Bullying

Cyberbullying is increasing on campus (Walker, Sockman, and Koehn 2011; Selkie, Fales, and Moreno 2016). It may be towards a person of a different race, or against someone who has a different political viewpoint or sexual preference. Activities like confronting someone; shaming them by posting potentially humiliating information; sending hate messages (e.g., email, texts, notes); or owning, distributing, or streaming any photos or videos of a person's private behavior are never okay and may be illegal. Such behavior can result in the bully being expelled. If your child is being bullied, or if they know someone else is being bullied, they need to report it.

How you can help your child deal with bullying

- Emphasize that it is important that your child should never be a bully and that they need to notify you and an advisor, therapist or mentor at school if they feel they are being bullied and/or if someone is secretly filming them or another student.

- Explain to your child how nothing online permanently disappears even if social media sites claim that it does. A classmate may ask to take a "funny" picture, claiming that it will disappear in seconds. Make sure that your child understands that the picture can "live" online indefinitely.

It's a matter of opinion: tolerating different perspectives

College is a place where different views are discussed, and students explore new ideas and social causes. A professor will often try to expose students to different perspectives. It is important students realize that having a different opinion is not an insult and does not mean that the other person thinks that a student is wrong.

Students with ASD often have a hard time differentiating between someone expressing a different opinion and a person trying to start an argument. This can be particularly challenging when an ASD student is exposed to a speaker who has a different point of view. It is important that students on the Spectrum realize that freedom of speech is a constitutional right. Your child does not have to agree with the speaker. They may ask a question or write about their perspective, but respecting different opinions is a crucial part of becoming an adult. If they feel a speaker's views are racist, insulting or inflammatory, they can disagree verbally or walk out peacefully. You should stress, however, that they should not respond aggressively.

How you can help your child respect different opinions

- Have a regular TV night where you and your child watch programs that express views different to yours, and role-play ways to respond.

- Bring life experiences to the dinner table. Describe how you felt about a situation and how you handled it.

- Together read articles that present different political issues and viewpoints.

- Review editorials to illustrate how common it is to encounter different opinions about a specific issue. Show that it does not necessarily mean that the two parties cannot be friends.

- Remind your child that people differ in the ways they disagree and cope. Some talk loudly, thinking that makes them seem stronger. Others are soft-spoken, preferring to avoid conflicts by not speaking up.

- If you love a family member who has very different opinions on certain issues, explain how you cope when these issues arise.

Self-advocacy

As mentioned earlier, because they are legally adults, students must apply for services themselves. To do this they must be open about their diagnosis with the appropriate people on campus.

Students on the Spectrum are often afraid to ask for help. In general, they fear that their classmates will learn about their diagnosis if they talk with their teacher or their RA and get accommodations. At one point in their schooling, they may have had a teacher who told the class about their diagnosis. They may also think that other students in the waiting areas at the student health center will focus on them, not recognizing that the other students also go there for help and are not concerned about why other people are there.

Students on the Spectrum probably did not know who in their high school had an IEP or saw a therapist, as they may have done. They were not aware that many of their classmates struggled with issues of their own. The students who are at risk of being expelled are not those who go for help. Rather the at-risk students are those who refuse offers of help.

For many college students, a big challenge is standing up for themselves. Steve described how he learned to do just that: "One of the big things mom taught me was that, in college, you have to focus on you. It was a big problem for me when I was trying to talk to the teacher. I would let people go ahead of me in line, and I would try not to waste the teacher's time, so I would rush my question and get nervous. I wish I had realized then that I'm important, that I'm paying to go here, and that I should look out for number one. That would have helped my confidence. I needed to say 'I need to speak with you now' and just follow the teacher around for a bit." Steve

How you can help your child become a self-advocate

- Remind your child that you think more highly of colleagues, family members, or students who seek help over those who criticize people for seeking support and then make serious mistakes.

- Remind your child how the help they received in school up to this point made them stronger and more confident.

- Underscore that college is hard for everyone. It demands more time, concentration and often more complex work than they have ever done before, on top of organizing their daily living. That is why colleges today make sure that they have many different ways for students to get support ranging from their RA, professors, the resource center, medical and mental health centers, and disability services if they applied and were accepted.

- Students who enlist the support of an empathetic professor, TA, or counselor are always ahead of students who escape into a sci-fi computer game or video. That type of coping never solves an issue.

Risky behaviors: drinking, drugs, and sex

College may be the first time students are exposed to high-risk behavior such as drinking, drugs, and sex. It is important students understand they do not have to do everything that their roommates or friends are doing, and that it is okay to leave a situation if they are uncomfortable.

Most schools require that all new students review policies regarding drugs, drinking, and sex. Many universities have mandatory online classes that the students must take on these subjects, either during orientation or some other time before school begins.

Drinking and drugs

Dangerous and underage drinking on college campuses is a significant public health problem that has taken an enormous toll on college students across the United States (White and Hingson 2013). Students often come to college with a drinking habit, which social pressure and college stress exacerbate. A national survey by the National Institute on Alcohol Abuse and Alcoholism found that almost 60 percent of college students aged 18 to 22 drank alcohol in the previous month and that almost two out of three of them engaged in binge drinking during the same timeframe (Substance Abuse & Mental Health Services Administration, or SAMHSA 2014). Orientation and Greek Rush weeks are known as times when students drink too much and risk serious emotional and physical injury.

Some students have been assaulted when they have had too much to drink or have experimented with dangerous drugs. Many have awakened hours later without remembering the assault or even earlier conversations. Newspapers describe court cases about assaults that occurred when a college student was under the influence of too much alcohol or given a drug in a drink by a "friend."

The best way to create safer campuses is a mix of individual- and environmental-level interventions that work to maximize positive outcomes. According to the National Institute on Alcohol Abuse and Alcoholism (NIAAA) (2015), change will not occur until college administrators limit drinking and drug use on all the private institutions on campuses, such as fraternities and sororities. Many universities now recommend women bring a buddy to any party where there will be drinking. The buddy will either abstain from drinking totally or limit intake (probably to one drink) to make sure their friend is okay.

Buddy or no buddy, it is essential that all students understand the serious dangers of drinking. You should discuss limits on alcohol consumption, especially binge drinking, with your child. The Mayo Clinic (2018) defines binge drinking as a male having five or more drinks within two hours, and a female having four drinks in that timeframe. Binge drinking can lead to alcoholic poisoning, which can be fatal.

Sex

Parents, physicians, and/or therapists need to review sexual assault and related issues with children before they go to college. Most schools require that students watch a video or take a seminar on this topic.

It is important that you review the concept of consent with your children. The consent must be verbal. It is never okay to force a person to have sex and consent cannot be given if a person is intoxicated. Many cases of sexual assault and abuse occur after the teens and adults first had alcohol and/or drugs.

You must stress that it is the responsibility of both consenting adults to make sure condoms are worn to protect against sexually transmitted diseases (STDs), which can have serious, lifelong consequences. Oral contraceptives provide additional protection to help prevent pregnancy.

Most college campuses offer self-defense courses, especially for women, teaching people how to protect themselves if they feel threatened. However, it's probably safe to assume that these skills won't be as effective if the student is under the influence of alcohol or drugs.

Awareness of others' risky behavior

Although students are mainly responsible for themselves, they should still care about others. If they think a friend or roommate is engaging in dangerous behavior that may hurt them or others (e.g., if the person is not going to meals, not talking to classmates, or making unrealistic demands), they should let their RA know.

If the RA is not available, the student can contact the school's 24-hour support or emergency number. (Most residential schools have a number that students can call if someone needs help.) The student could also call that number or the campus police if they are worried that a friend or roommate drank too much at a party. You should emphasize the fact that friends will always be grateful if someone prevents them from hurting themselves (even though the friends might not realize it at the time).

NOTE

When students call because they are concerned about a friend in need of help, they are generally not held legally responsible for the friend's situation. This is called the Good Samaritan Law (Drug Policy Alliance). The RA should know how the school handles such situations. Most schools have online rules that they make each student watch and sign during orientation.

How you can help your child resist risky behaviors

- Discuss the topics of drinking, drugs, sex and STDs with your child. Share your views and ask them to articulate theirs, so they have time to think about the issues before encountering these situations.

- Check the university's website to find out what type of education they give students about risky behaviors. Also check the university's rules related to these issues.

The first six months

The first six months of college are generally the most difficult time for many students, especially those who were heavily dependent on parents or other adults for support. For some, it is the first time they experience a significant separation from home and are exposed to people from different races, religions, and lifestyles. It is also a time when students are invited to parties where alcohol and other substances are readily available.

Many of these students turn to their parents for daily support rather than their RAs or peers. The students may feel that other kids do not like them, especially if they did not have positive social experiences in high school.

You and your child will have to come to terms with your new communication relationship. Before the your child goes to college, it's good to discuss how, and how often, they will communicate with you.

> One father described how his son, Thomas, would call him often during the freshman year, saying he had to leave: "He said he couldn't make it. He couldn't handle it. So I'd go down and buy him a cup of coffee, just talk him off the ledge. He didn't have a lot of friends in high school, and so we would talk about things. I was like his best friend and listening post. And I would ask him: 'How did they build the pyramids? They put one brick up at a time. All you have to worry about is the next brick. Your brain is going too fast and you're thinking about the whole situation.' I would calm him down and get him to think incrementally." Mark, Thomas's father

This college generation relates well to texts, so a few texts and a phone call each week are often enough. Too many texts and calls, and the student might not adjust properly to college life.

Of course, many parents will worry about their children and may be shocked to learn that schools are generally restricted as to how much information they can share about the children.

Most medical clinics will meet with parents and their children during orientation or when they move onto campus. Fortunately, many schools inform parents ahead of time about the HIPAA laws and give them a consent form to complete at the start of the year that allows school officials to contact the parents if they are concerned about the student's academic performance or health. Chapter 2 has more information about communication restrictions.

As one mother explained: "We told him that his first semester was a learning curve just like any new school or a job would be and he was doing fine. Parents need to be supportive and remember that it's four times harder for those kids than for kids who are not on the Spectrum. Being supportive of their academic and social life is important, while not hovering over them. They are adults and want to be treated as such. They want to feel that the parents are not controlling their lives, even if they are paying for the school. We had him pay a certain amount for each class he takes and, if he passes the class with a C or better, we roll the money to the next semester. Otherwise we keep it. We felt that it was a way for him to feel accountable for his success. We are aware that some academic advisors tell the students that they need to take a full load of classes but it is important that the students realize it is not essential to do it their first year of college." Mandy

How you can help your child adjust in the first six months

- Determine, in advance, how often you will reach out to your child while in college, and what form that communication will take. Are weekly phone calls enough? Texts? What about FaceTime or Skype?

- Encourage your child to grant permission for the academic and mental health staff to contact you if the school is concerned.

- If you do not hear from your child for more than one week, check in. They may be involved in an activity and forgot to let you know ahead of time. Keep your cool and remember how many times they forgot to call when they were out with friends at home.

- Some college students will not call if they fear you are mad at them for not calling earlier. Remind yourself it's important to keep your communication supportive if you want to maintain it later.

- Remind your child that many students find it challenging to balance day-to-day living, schoolwork, and a personal life at first. However, that feeling may pass after they develop a new routine. If they are still feeling that way after their first exams, encourage them to talk with a mental health professional in the student services. Recognize that the professional may recommend a comprehensive psychological evaluation.

- Remember that positive encouragement is always better than threats.

KEY POINTS

» Virtually all students experience some stress and uncertainty while adjusting to college. These experiences are especially acute for students on the Spectrum.

» Many ASD students resist using the services offered at their college because they think they do not need them or want to appear "normal."

» Students, especially those on the Spectrum, may have problems interpreting social cues and making new friends.

» Social communication challenges include respecting different opinions.

» College may be the first time students are exposed to risky behaviors such as drinking, drugs, and sex.

» The first six months are typically the hardest time both for students and their parents.

Recap of how you can help
How you can help your child manage stress

- Share the activities that calm you down such as deep breathing, muscle stretching, taking a walk, or listening to a favorite song or a meditation app.

- Help your child identify ways they find effective to reduce stress before there is a crisis, such as physical activities, games, artistic expression, meditation, yoga, or talking with a friend.

- Help your child manage interruptions.

- Encourage your child to give the school's academic and mental health staff permission to contact you if there is a concern.

- Help your child create a plan for obtaining emotional support through the school health office, a therapist, or support group.

How you can help your child socialize and make friends

- Discuss with your child what it was like for you when you met your freshman year college roommate. Were they from a different state or country? Could you understand them or did they have a strong accent? Did you have shared interests? Did you have meals, classes or participate in school activities together? You can point out that sometimes it is nice to have someone to talk with even if you did not see them very often during the day.

- While your child is in high school, encourage participation in clubs, teams and other social groups, so that they get used to interacting with others in different environments.

- Encourage your child to participate in a freshman orientation program as a way of meeting other college students.

- Encourage your child to consider support groups and other special-interest groups that may help them find friends with shared interests.

How you can help your child deal with bullying

- Emphasize that it is important that your child should never be a bully and that they need to notify you and an advisor, therapist or mentor at school if they feel they are being bullied and/or if someone is secretly filming them or another student.

- Explain to your child how nothing online permanently disappears even if social media sites claim that it does.

How you can help your child
respect different opinions

- Make dinner a time when your children feel safe to express different views on issues related to current school, community, national and international news, popular computer games, and videos.

- Share with your child examples of how you handled working with colleagues, and being around friends who had different views towards issues that were important to you.

- Remind your child that when family members gather to celebrate a holiday it is common, as with college, to spend time with others who may have strong feelings about certain issues, which are very different from yours. Describe how you have handled these situations, emphasizing that even when there was a strong disagreement on an issue or idea the best approach involved listening to and respecting the opinions and feelings of others. The priority was not to prove the superiority of one view but rather to stay positive and make the event pleasurable for all participants. Reassure them that there will be other time to discuss any frustrations in a more private setting.

- Remind your child that people differ in the ways they disagree and cope.

- If a family member has very different opinions on certain issues, explain how you cope when these issues arise.

How you can help your child become a self-advocate

- Be sensitive to how you speak about mental health issues in adolescents. If teens fear that others may be critical of them for seeking mental health support then they may choose to avoid it.

- Underscore that college can be hard for everyone in the beginning. It demands more time, concentration, and often more complex work than they have ever done before, on top of organizing their daily living.

How you can help your child resist risky behaviors

- If you have had mental health support that helped you be a better parent, you can share that and point out that their support system, similarly, helped them be a better student and friend.

- Check the university's website to find out what how the schools educate students about school legal and ethical rules pertaining to drugs, sex, and harassment.

How you can help your child adjust during the first six months

- Determine, in advance and jointly, how often you will reach out to your child while in college, and what form that communication may take. Are weekly phone calls enough? Texts? What about FaceTime or Skype?

- Encourage your child to grant permission for the academic and mental health staff to contact you if the school is concerned.

- If you do not hear from your child for more than two weeks, check in. They may be involved in an activity and forgot to let you know ahead of time.

- Some college students will not call if they fear you will be critical of them. It's important to keep your communication supportive if you want to maintain it.

- Remind your child that many students find it challenging to balance day-to-day living, schoolwork, and a personal life at first. If they experience persistent negative feelings, they may benefit from talking with a mental health professional in the student services.

- Remember that positive encouragement is always better than threats.

— Chapter 5 —

Mental Health Issues

Historically the fact that students on the Spectrum could also suffer from mental health disorders largely went unnoticed. That started to change in 2013 when the American Psychiatric Association published the fifth edition of the *Diagnostic and Statistical Manual of Mental Disorders (DSM-5)*, which permits multiple diagnoses. With this shift comes a growing awareness that college students on the Spectrum may also suffer from mental health disorders.

The goal of this chapter is to help you better understand ASD and the most common mental health issues your child might face. Specifically, we'll discuss these common disorders and their treatment options:

- ADHD

- anxiety disorders

- depression

- suicidal ideation

- bipolar disorder

- obsessive-compulsive disorder

- obsessive-compulsive and related disorders

- schizophrenia.

Increasing numbers of students with mental health issues are going to college. Some psychiatric disabilities are more common than others among these students. A 2012 National Alliance on Mental Illness (NAMI) survey titled "College Students Speak" noted that:

- 27 percent of all respondents (male and female) said they lived with depression

- 24 percent said they lived with bipolar disorder

- 12 percent said they lived with "other conditions," including dysthymia (persistent depressive disorder), eating disorders, and obsessive-compulsive disorder (OCD)

- 11 percent said they lived with anxiety

- 6 percent said they lived with schizophrenia

- 5 percent said they lived with Attention Deficit Hyperactivity Disorder (ADHD)

- 1 percent said they lived with substance abuse.

So, many students enter college with mental health issues, or experience them for the first time in college. In the case of ASD students, the challenge of managing day-to-day life without the support of family, and the stress of college life, often gives rise to an increase in symptoms associated with managing ADHD, anxiety, OCD, depression, bipolar disorder, and schizophrenia.

Here are the most common disorders college students, including those on the Spectrum, experience. Part of this information is derived from Autism Speaks.[1]

---

1   www.autismspeaks.org

ASD and ADHD

ADHD affects 30 to 60 percent of people on the Spectrum. It is often the primary diagnosis given to children by clinicians who are not experienced in evaluating such students. ADHD entails a persistent pattern of inattention, and difficulty managing daily responsibilities and larger school projects. The hyperactivity/impulsivity interferes with learning, social relationships, and the overall quality of daily life. Research has shown that medication is the most effective treatment for ADHD. Students may also benefit from social-skills training, cognitive-behavioral therapy, and academic and organizational assistance.

Many of the students discussed in this book were initially diagnosed as having ADHD when they were in elementary school and diagnosed as being on the Spectrum in middle school, high school, or college.

ASD and anxiety disorders

Anxiety affects up to 42 percent of people with ASD. By contrast it affects an estimated 15 percent of the general population (Autism Speaks). Individuals on the Spectrum have trouble assessing and expressing how they feel, often resulting in an emotional meltdown or withdrawal from a stressful situation. They may misread others as being critical of them or be overwhelmed by loud sounds or other sensory stimuli in their dorm or on the campus. Many individuals who cannot identify their distress describe physical manifestations such as a racing heart, muscle and stomach tightness or headaches. Others may feel immobilized or feel compelled to find a safe private place.

Common traits of ASD students, such as challenges with time management, can make the students more anxious. Zoe, who described her time-management challenges in

Chapter 3, is often depressed and anxious, which adversely affects her health. This undermines her ability to complete work on time which, in turn, makes her more anxious and depressed.

ASD and depression

Depression affects an estimated 26 percent of adolescents and adults on the Spectrum, compared to an estimated 7 percent of the general population. The rate of depression increases with age and cognitive ability. The difficulty in communication associated with ASD may at times be confused with depression, when individuals seem to shut down and have difficulty explaining how they feel (Autism Speaks). Typical symptoms include:

- a loss of interest in activities they were once passionate about, such as a favorite computer game, class, sport, or club

- a loss of appetite; a breakdown in daily hygiene; feelings of sadness, hopelessness, and irritability

- at its most serious, thoughts of death and suicide.

"In high school my son had a group of close friends who were probably forgiving. I think several of them were on the Spectrum themselves, and they all became very insular in high school. Later, when I picked him up for spring break, he was really sad and told me about his depression, saying, 'I know that I am different but I did not realize how different I am.'" Joan, Gabe's mother

---

Depression is often a taboo subject. In a book about his father's depression, Dr. Hinshaw, a psychology professor, revealed that his family had an "enforced silence" about his father's diagnosis. The taboo associated with talking about their father stopped the family from expressing their feelings of anxiety, anger, and sadness associated with their father's unpredictable behavior and hospitalizations. His personal experiences motivated Dr. Hinshaw to develop a clinical research program for students with mental health disorders (Hinshaw 2017).

ASD and suicidal ideation

A study of more than 5000 members of the United Kingdom–based birth cohort study of the Avon Longitudinal Study of Parents and Children provides insights into ASD traits and suicidal thoughts, plans, and self-harm in late adolescence.

They found a relationship between thoughts of suicide and impaired social communication, but did not find a connection with any other key autism traits. And a significant part of the association between social communication impairment and self-harm was explained by depression rather than by autism (Culpin *et al.* 2018).

Jackson *et al.* (2018) collected data from their online survey of college students with ASD. Nearly 75 percent of those who responded to the questions related to suicidal behavior had reported some form of suicidal behavior (plans or attempts) in their lifetimes. More than 53 percent of the respondents had thought about suicide within the previous year and almost 18 percent of the respondents reported that it was "likely" or "very likely" that they would attempt suicide someday. The factors that the respondents found to be significantly associated with the risk of these thoughts were the number of friends; their overall loneliness; academic comfort; and symptoms of depression, anxiety, and stress.

In other surveys of college students on the Spectrum, participants reported being generally comfortable with the academic demands, but struggling with feelings of isolation and loneliness, stress, anxiety, depression, and an increased incidence of dropping out. White *et al.* 2011 reported on the growing number of students with these diagnoses not being identified until they were enrolled in college. They went on to discuss how the needs of students are diverse—outlining many of the issues previously discussed in this book such as difficulty with time management, self-advocacy, isolation, and loneliness. They also noted that the higher functioning students were often more aware of others bullying or avoiding them. Not surprisingly they also scored higher in the areas of depression, anxiety, and aggressive behavior. The study underlines the need for college programs to be attentive to both the academic disabilities and mental health issues of high functioning college students on the autism spectrum.

This makes it all the more important that parents of teenagers who have had suicidal thoughts discuss ways the child could cope should those thoughts reoccur. For example, most schools have a 24/7 helpline. They can contact their therapist and tell the answering service that it is an emergency. They could ask a friend or roommate to walk them to the health center if they cannot go by themselves. They can call the student police who generally will drive them to the health service or contact the health center.

Parents should also find out the school's policy regarding these types of situations. Does the school expel the student or does the school support hospitalization and incorporating them back into the school pending their therapist's recommendations? Universities have been sued for how they have handled these situations with a lack of attention to the students' mental health or academic issues. Some have started programs that are more attentive to identifying and intervening with the precipitating factors contributing to the students' feelings of loneliness and helplessness.

A growing number of schools force the student to leave the school and get therapy offsite. For legal reasons, if the student returns to school, they often have to sign a form that absolves the school of any responsibility if they commit suicide.

"In the beginning, everything was good but things got hard for me in the winter quarter. Both semesters went well for me academically, but the non-academic things didn't work out. I couldn't get my interview together; I didn't get any of the things (clubs and activities) I applied for, and I lost a big student-government election after winning the first round.

I thought that just nothing was going to work out for me because I have this disorder. One night I hit rock bottom. I didn't attempt suicide but I got what was necessary for it. As soon as I realized that I was acting that way, I threw the stuff away, got into the fetal position, told someone, and signed up for counseling." Thomas

How you can help your child cope with suicidal thoughts

- Talk with your child and discuss ways he or she could handle this type of crisis. Identify resources such as a therapist or other advisors should these feelings arise.

- Make sure your child has the college's emergency number so that he or she could call when they need to speak to someone right away. The number is often posted online as well as on their RA's door.

- Check to see if there is an online support system.

- If your child has had suicidal thoughts in the past, find out the school's policy toward this. Do they hospitalize the students and incorporate them back into the school pending their therapist's recommendations or do they expel them?

ASD and OCD

OCD commonly begins in adolescence and early adulthood. For students on the Spectrum it can sometimes be hard to differentiate the disorder from an area of restricted interest or repetitive behavior such as watching a favorite YouTube video over and over again. There is a growing interest in the similarities between the special interests of individuals on the Autism Spectrum and obsessive compulsive behavior (Yuhas 2019).

People with an OCD condition that goes beyond what is typically seen in ASD often:

- have repeated thoughts, images and urges about different issues including being compulsively neat and organized, fearing germs and dirt, or avoiding public pools on campus and public beaches

- incessantly fear intruders or personal violence, imagine hurting a loved one, or imagine behaving in ways that conflict with their religious beliefs

- engage in repetitive behaviors such as washing their hands, locking and unlocking doors, counting, writing numbers, or hoarding unneeded items.

This disorder can have a prolonged negative impact on students who think their fears are justified and resist getting help. However, students who get support for their OCD condition may see benefits quickly. It is important to realize that, while OCD behaviors are not rational, trying to abolish them by explaining to the student that the behavior is irrational does not help.

Two possible treatments that often do work are cognitive behavioral therapy (CBT) and exposure therapy. CBT is a type of talk psychotherapy. The student works with the therapist in a structured way for a limited number of sessions.

The goal is to help the student become aware of inaccurate or negative perceptions or thinking, and develop more adaptable ways to perceive and deal with these challenging situations. CBT has also been recommended when medication has not been successful, or in some situations with medication. This type of therapy may be provided individually or as part of a support group.

Exposure therapy utilizes small steps of exposing the client to things or situations that they cannot tolerate or are afraid of, such as touching, going on a plane, or using a computer if they fear that it is contaminated. Medication and exposure therapy are sometimes helpful together in these areas. Notably, most students who are motivated are able to utilize exposure therapy and realize, for example, that their computer or phone does not need to be sanitized every time they use it or bring it into their dorm room. The same exposure therapy techniques can help students move towards eating in the cafeteria, working in the library, or attending small social events.

ASD and obsessive-compulsive and related disorders (OCRDs)

A new diagnostic category in *DSM-5* is obsessive-compulsive and related disorders, which includes an "other-specified" and "unspecified" diagnosis. This group of disorders includes individuals who have OCD features that cause significant stress and impairment, but the individuals do not meet all the criteria for an OCD diagnosis.

For example, students might bite their nails excessively, pick their skin, or have obsessive thoughts about how they look. They may be envious of classmates who get more positive stars or hearts on their posts. These obsessive thoughts are a form of OCD but do not meet the full criteria for the diagnosis. The diagnosis may apply to a person for whom the behavior may be a side effect of a medication (Zupanick 2014).

"There's this weird Asperger's curse of having a fraction of OCD, but not enough to be classified as OCD. I love to have everything organized, like my books. My wife and I share bookshelves and we still have books up in my Mom's attic. My desk looks amazing; my medicine cabinet is splendiferous, but I can't keep track of a calendar for the life of me. It's the real-world things. I have an app called the mindfulness bell. I set it to go off a set number of times. It reminds me to get up, get ready for school and my class schedule." Daniel

ASD and schizophrenia

Unlike ASD, schizophrenia is often seen for the first time in adolescents and adults in their early 20s. Both disorders involve communication challenges and occasionally there are instances where ASD-like symptoms, including social impairments and unusual beliefs, precede a diagnosis of schizophrenia. However, schizophrenia often includes hallucinations, delusions, and/or being cognitively disconnected from objective reality.

Medication is generally the most effective treatment for schizophrenia.

KEY POINTS

» Only recently has it been accepted that a person on the Spectrum can also have other mental health disorders.

» All the mental health disorders prevalent in students on the Spectrum are also seen in the broader college student population.

» Colleges need to view mental health as a central part of their students' experience. Too often the focus is solely on academic performance.

Recap of how you can help your child cope with suicidal thoughts

- During orientation stop by the student health and disability services and learn about the best way to get support on campus. Remind them that they can always call 911 if they are feeling at all that they might hurt themselves.

- Encourage your child to participate in the types of activities that helped them in high school when they were feeling depressed or overwhelmed such as yoga, meditation, a walking group, or finding either an onsite therapist or clinician in the community. Also see if there is an existing support group or community service program that may provide a support network when they feel alone.

- If your child has had suicidal thoughts in the past, find out the school's policy toward such behavior.

- Remember that your child may be doing well academically and still struggling with other emotional and social issues. The opposite can sometimes be true.

— Chapter 6 —

Mental Health Services in Today's Colleges

Most state universities, colleges, and community colleges are required by law to provide services for students with disabilities and mental health issues. However, this does not guarantee that they have enough staff—or the right staff— to meet the growing demands of their student population. The key issue is how much the school makes student mental health services a priority.

In this chapter we will discuss:

- common services and accommodations

- considerations for parents

- evaluating services

- the future of college and support services

- the stepped model

- special programs for high-functioning students on the Spectrum

- before applying for special programs

- how you can help.

The growing need for mental health services on college campuses has become an urgent issue for colleges throughout the country. This has been tragically demonstrated by the fact that most of the college students who committed suicide had never sought help. In a recent study, more than 80 percent of the students who committed suicide had never set foot in the health clinic. That study tracked more than 43,000 undergraduates and found that one-third of them demonstrated significant symptoms of a mental health problem such as depression, generalized anxiety, substance abuse, or suicidal ideation over a period of six years (Ketchen Lipson *et al.* 2015).

However, nationally only about 11 percent of students in need of mental health services seek help (Ketchen Lipson *et al.* 2015). This may be changing, as recent research indicates that more students are seeking help. The number of students seeking appointments at counseling centers rose 30 percent between the 2009/10 and 2014/15 timeframes, even though the student population increased only 5 percent in that timeframe. This may be the result of outreach efforts to identify at-risk students and to encourage parents to seek professional help either at the school or in the community.

Of those seeking therapy, 61 percent reported having anxiety. Other major issues reported were depression (49 percent), stress (45 percent), family issues (31 percent), academic performance (28 percent), and relationship problems (27 percent) (Center for Collegiate Mental Health 2016).

Colleges vary dramatically in the extent of disability services they provide for all high-functioning students, especially those with ASD. Students with high grades often do not qualify for disability services. Mental health issues are often ignored as well, if it appears the issues do not impact a student's academic performance—unless, of course, the behavior puts the student or others at risk. (Schools generally pay attention if students pose a risk of hurting themselves or others, which increases the school's potential liability.)

Since the students are legally adults, they are the only ones who can disclose their diagnoses and past interventions, and ask for disability services. The challenge for students on the Spectrum is that, in their desire to fit in and "look normal," they avoid the very services that could smooth their transition to college life. They often overlook the fact that they will participate in all the same classes as their peers. The programs simply help level the playing field so that they can work to the best of their ability. Typically, the programs provide a variety of different services such as an advisor to help the students select courses, organize their academic day, arrange tutoring if needed, and connect them with mental health services and social support groups. Some programs connect students on the Spectrum with a college buddy who orients the new student to the world of the college campus.

The students I know who were asked to leave their colleges had refused to seek academic and mental health help. One had parents who guided him in going to the disability or mental health services on campus. They wrote a detailed letter describing their child's diagnosis, medication, and prior mental health services, but these attempts were fruitless since their child did not seek help. Instead the child was on the computer around the clock playing computer games and gambling. Teachers and student services tried to arrange meetings with him, but he did not respond. Eventually he was asked to leave the college.

> The mother of a client described how her son avoided getting services. "I thought he signed up for services with his father but his dad did not wait for him to be interviewed because there was a long line. The plan was for Gabe to follow through with it, but he did not. I think that when he did his application he listed his diabetes, but not his Autism Spectrum Disorder or Asperger's Disorder." Joan, Gabe's mother

Common services and accommodations

Over the last several years colleges have begun paying more attention to suicide rates, and alcohol and drug abuse. For these reasons, colleges are beginning to look beyond the traditional mental health models, with services located on one site, to ways the colleges can better reach out to students who need help but aren't actively seeking it.

That said, there is no guarantee that any particular type of college—be it a high-ranking university, a small private college or a large community college—will be able to meet the overall demand for services, or meet your child's specific needs. Nor is there any guarantee that your child will qualify for services, even if he or she qualified in high school. (The process of applying for services is covered in Chapter 2.)

Often school mental health programs are based on special private funding. For instance, the Schwab Foundation funds programs for tutoring and learning differences. Many of these programs provide services for students with ADHD, as either a primary or co-diagnosis. Such programs are popular partially because they do not have the stigma of a mental health or disability services program.

Here are some of the more common mental health and disability accommodations and services that colleges provide:

- allowing students to complete coursework, give presentations, and take exams in alternative formats

- providing access to adaptive software and technologies that can help the students learn and work more productively

- appointing note-takers, readers, scribes, and the like

- allowing extra time for assignments and tests as well as providing help getting to class

- providing assistive technology such as electronic planners, digital recorders for blind students, and special hearing technology for deaf students (colleges are increasingly providing these assistive technologies to students who cannot afford them)

- guiding students with disabilities to specialized counselors, resource centers, and other on-campus services

- offering wellbeing programs that, among other benefits, help students deal with stress, anxiety, and physical health

- facilitating peer-run support groups.

Note that the disability specialists at most colleges do not help students with schoolwork. Your child will not be entitled to any more tutoring hours than any other student. Nor can your child be tutored one-on-one unless all students have that option. (Some colleges will provide additional tutoring for a fee.) A useful resource is the College Guide for Students with Psychiatric Disabilities on the Best Colleges website.[1]

Even when students apply for services, they must be prepared to wait. Nationwide, a 2016 survey found that, on average, 1737 students were seeking help for every available staff person. Smaller institutions (with fewer than 1500 students) had smaller ratios, on average 705 to 1, while larger schools (more than 35,000 students) had much larger ratios, on average 2624 to 1 according to The Association for University and College Counseling Center Directors Annual Survey (LeViness, Bershad, and Gorman, reporting period 7/1/16 to 6/30/17).

---

1   www.bestcolleges.com/resources/college-planning-with-psychiatric-disabilities

These findings underscore the need to find new ways to reach out to college students and make mental health services a more common part of the college experience. Otherwise the high number of students in need of help will either drop out of college or find more destructive "coping" strategies such as alcohol, drugs, or suicide.

These findings are basically true for all colleges except those with programs that are designed for students on the Spectrum. Two such programs are described at the end of this chapter.

On a positive note, many college students are being more assertive and demanding that their school increase the number of quality mental health professionals with expertise in the problem areas often seen on college campuses such as depression, anxiety, alcohol abuse, anorexia, learning differences, medical issues, physical disabilities, and ASD. These students are also asking that the services be more easily accessible.

Some colleges are supporting more extensive programs. A growing trend in those cases is to have enough trained staff available to ensure that a college student can quickly get an appointment if they are experiencing a crisis. The stepped model, described later in this chapter, provides an organizational framework for expediting help where it is most needed.

Considerations for parents

As already stated, it's essential to evaluate the school's mental health services as well as its academic offerings. However, before that step, it is important to evaluate your child's situation for factors such as:

- Is your child aware that many college students do not like to be identified by mental health issues?

- Is your child willing to let the college know that he or she is on the Spectrum? (As illustrated by the cases presented in this book, high-functioning students on the Spectrum often do not want to be identified as having special needs.)

- Is your child willing to participate in a support program for ASD students?

- Does your insurance cover student mental health services or will you need to enroll your child in the university medical plan to qualify?

- Is your child aware that he or she will have to initiate getting services? (The more prepared your child is, the more likely he or she will get that help.)

- Is your child fully aware of the extent of special support they have already received from the school, outside tutors, therapists, and you?

Evaluating services

It's hard to find special programs for students with ASD and mental health issues. That's why parents need to research whether the school provides special services for high-functioning students on the Spectrum *before* applying to the college. Those services may be more important to your child's success than any academic program.

Chapter 2 listed some areas to consider in evaluating schools in general. It's also particularly important to consider the expertise of the staff to make sure that your child can get the kind of help he or she needs. However, if your child needs medication, make sure the school has a psychiatrist on staff.

Here is a summary of the kinds of services mental health professionals provide:

- Psychiatrists prescribe medication and may see clients as infrequently as every three months. They may also provide individual therapy and supervise psychiatry fellows and psychology interns.

- Psychologists may do diagnostic testing, individual and group therapy, and supervise psychology interns.

- Social workers and counselors typically do therapy. They may also provide wellbeing services and organize support groups, which were mentioned earlier in this chapter.

NOTE

In a recent survey, more than half of the centers had a full- or part-time psychiatric provider in the counseling center. However, almost 65 percent of directors who had a psychiatrist said that they need more hours of psychiatric services than they currently have (The Association for University and College Counseling Centers Directors Annual Survey, 2016).

Fortunately, there is now a greater awareness of the need for specially trained mental health professionals to work with college-age students. No standardized models currently exist for the training of the psychiatrists, psychologists and social workers who care for this population. However, it is widely accepted that there is a need for a more comprehensive mental health approach that includes the students' development, age of onset, family history, and comorbidities. When appropriate, this approach should include the parents as well. The programs need to look at both problem prevention and retention of students with overt mental health and developmental issues (Riba *et al.* 2015).

Ideally, colleges will adopt this systems approach, which encompasses all areas of the students' lives. This approach moves beyond looking at the individual in isolation. Instead it looks at the student in the context of the larger system—the family, the campus (including the students' living situation, roommates, teachers and administration) and the larger community. Looking at these levels as a whole, increases understanding of the issues, and helps professionals develop interventions that address relevant factors.

The future of college and support services

As we discussed, many studies have shown that more students are experiencing mental health issues in college. This illustrates the need for colleges to view mental health as a central part of the students' experience. All too often colleges and universities focus solely on academic performance.

What is needed is a systems approach or program that supports the student individually as well as in the context of their relationships with their peers, teachers, and community settings such as religious organizations, community service programs or work, e.g., an internship (Bronfenbrenner 1981).

The next chapter will discuss the types of services available for students with mental health issues, and address the need for college services to be more attuned to the impact that the students' mental health plays in their adaptation to college. More information on college programs designed to help children adjust to the social as well as academic demands of college is included in the Further Reading section of this book.

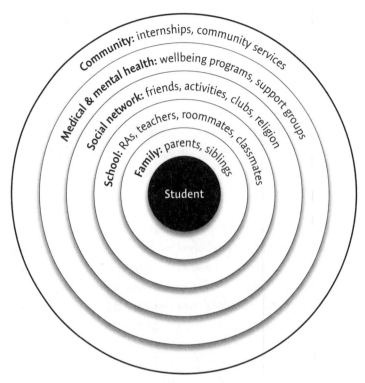

College students' mental health and wellbeing: a systems approach

The stepped model

Cornish and colleagues (2017) propose a model for addressing the increased demands for mental health services at colleges that have limited funds and staff. Their stepped model addresses different mental health issues based on the level of services that the student needs.

The model addresses the complexity of many mental health disorders, stressing the lack of response to short-term therapy and the fact that these students may be very sensitive to medication and require more than 10-minute sessions with the medication provider.

This stepped model organizes programming in a diverse and client-sensitive manner. It starts with a client walk-in system. The clinicians should be well-rounded and have experience with a wide range of clients.

- Step 1 is online informational self-help. Students are encouraged to access the college's wellbeing site, which provides daily ideas for strategies in coping, such as exercise and diet, and information about other support on campus.

- Step 2 is online interactive workbooks that provide therapeutic models of Cognitive Behavior Therapy (CBT) and mindfulness, tools that have been found to help students who are not yet ready for therapy (or may not need therapy).

- Step 3 is interactive online psychoeducational sessions. WellTrack is one tool.[2] More than 50 different campuses are using this combined online and app-based technology.

- Step 4 is therapist-assisted mental health services for students with moderate to severe symptoms and high readiness. This level includes a variety of professional and peer-facilitated workshops. The sessions may focus on coping strategies and organization skills. The sessions may also provide support for students who do not feel included in other services, such as LGBTQA students, those with the stress of student loans or family stressors such as residency status, or students on the Spectrum who did not qualify for disability services and do not feel included in the peer mental health groups.

---

2 www.welltrack.com

- Step 5 consists of therapist-assisted online services for students with moderate-to-high symptoms, who have low-to-high readiness and are low-to-moderate risk. The services include evidence-based treatment for anxiety and depression.

- Step 6 is traditional face-to-face group therapy for students with moderate-to-high symptoms who have high readiness and low-to-moderate risk.

- Step 7 is for one-to-one counseling or individual therapy. The students need to be ready for the challenges associated with exploring the feelings, thoughts, and issues that they have been struggling with. The therapists are encouraged to use time wisely, but can see their clients on a more long-term basis if necessary. Some clients are seen for 20 to 50 minutes on a weekly basis, and others may move to weekly check-ins with their therapist. The program encourages its therapists to refer clients with more severe issues to therapists in the community who can see them for a longer period of time. Some schools have affiliated community mental health professionals who see students for a limited number of sessions for free.

- Step 8 includes outpatient psychiatric consultation for students with follow-up care provided by community therapists or family physicians.

- Step 9 is the highest level of intervention. It includes health system navigation, intensive case management, and crisis support for students with chronic conditions, substance abuse, behavioral violations, and suicidal ideation. Some of these students require hospitalization. Most have case coordinators who work collaboratively with the external services.

Lastly, Cornish suggests students on the Spectrum often benefit from having a paid or volunteer buddy who helps them deal with the campus social activities.

In follow-up evaluations, students on this stepped approach commented that they liked the fast response and "having a plan." However, implementing such a program requires major shifts in traditional training at all levels.

Special programs for high-functioning students on the Spectrum

Fortunately, some programs specifically designed for high-functioning students on the Spectrum follow the systems approach. These programs typically provide comprehensive services that support the students' academic and personal lives. For example, staff members help with housing and dorm issues; TAs help with course selections; counselors deal with daily course schedules; mental health professionals focus on specific mental health issues; and teachers who understand the ASD learning differences develop ways to help students adjust to their classes. Most of these programs also have a staff member and resource center to help arrange summer internships. These programs often have a separate application process that can be found on the college's website.

Two programs with excellent reputations for high-functioning college students on the Spectrum are Marshall University's College Program for Students with Autism Spectrum Disorders and Pace University's OASIS College Support Program.

Marshall University

Marshall University's College Program for Students with Autism Spectrum Disorders in Huntington, West Virginia, uses a positive behavioral support approach to help enrolled students. It offers academic support, social-skills support, and independent-living skills support.

The students must meet the acceptance criteria to be admitted to the program. The acceptance process consists of a written application and interview. A student's social, communication, academic, leisure and personal living skills are assessed through a personal planning session with the student, family members, and a member of the support staff.

The program's team includes faculty members, staff and mentors, all of whom receive training related to ASD. This training emphasizes the unique characteristics of each student and how that may impact their learning styles and social interactions.

Once accepted, students are paired with an older student. This buddy may show the new student around campus, share a meal, take the new student to a social event, help the new student evaluate possible activities, and introduce the freshman to their friends. The buddies are there to help new students adjust to the school.

For more information visit the school's website.[3]

Pace University—OASIS College Support Program

Pace University's Ongoing Academic Social Instructional Support (OASIS) program was started by a group of parents in New York who were concerned about the lack of programs that met their children's challenges and capitalized on their strengths. The group connected through their involvement in Autism Speaks.[4]

OASIS has a comprehensive support program for students with high-functioning autism and other learning differences. The program's team includes:

---

3   www.marshall.edu/collegeprogram
4   www.autismspeaks.org

- an academic coach, who meets with a student for one hour a day to help them manage their assignments and classes

- the internship coordinator, who works with Pace's career services and other university services to help the students find internships that meet their areas of interest

- the educational coordinator, who helps the student with course selection and registration

- the social worker, who provides social and emotional support, either individually or in a group

- the housing coordinator, who helps the students navigate residential and campus life (the coordinators are aware that these students tend to live on campus in isolation, escaping into their favorite computer game or online diversion); the housing coordinator's goal is to help incorporate the students into campus life through trips, activities, and participation in clubs

- the social coach, who teaches the students "social literacy" during the summer (social literacy entails learning how to read the verbal and non-verbal cues other people give you)

- the social coordinator, who helps students integrate into social activities at OASIS and at Pace.

Students on the Spectrum may also receive accommodations for testing and assignments, and Autism Speaks,[5] an autism advocacy organization, provides training and support for teachers who have these students in their classes. However, the OASIS students are Pace students first, and take the

---

5   www.autismspeaks.org

same challenging classes as their peers. While they do receive accommodations, their coursework must be at the college level.

Pace University is ranked as the top private, four-year college in the nation for upward economic mobility by Harvard University's Opportunity Insights.[6] The school has three campuses in New York: in New York City, Pleasantville, and White Plains.[7]

Also, the *Spectrum Support* Program provides innovative support that positively impacts the college experience for RIT (Rochester Institute of Technology) students, particularly those with ASD. The organization is committed to helping students build the connections to RIT that will help them achieve academic, social and career success.[8]

Before applying for special programs

Here are some questions to consider before your child applies to this type of program:

- How do you and your child feel about programs specifically for college students on the Spectrum?

- Does the school require special applications for the ASD program?

- Does the student need to qualify for disability services first?

- If choosing a specialized program, how well established is it? What is its reputation?

- What resources does the college provide in terms of:

---

6   www.opportunityinsights.org

7   www.pace.edu/oasis

8   https://www.rit.edu/studentaffairs/ssp/overview

- academic and organizational support?

- social support from campus volunteers and from peers in the program?

- adaptive campus living arrangements?

- training and support of the students' professors and advisors?

- collaboration with campus mental health providers?

- sharing the same goals in terms of your child having full inclusion in classes that fit the school's requirements and your child's interests, strengths and challenges?

The Further Reading section lists websites that give more information on the best college programs for high-functioning students on the Spectrum. However, none of the programs list the accommodations and services provided for students who have comorbidity with other mental health or medical disorders. One reason for this may be that ASD has typically been seen as a neurodevelopmental disorder. Only with *DSM-5* is ASD described as having comorbidity with other diagnoses.

KEY POINTS

» The school's mental health services may be more important for your child's success than the school's academic rankings or offerings.

» Colleges are required to provide some mental health services. However, the quality, quantity, and availability of those services may vary dramatically between institutions.

» Disability services generally provide assistance for students on the Spectrum as well as for others in the general student population.

» Students may not apply for disability services until they are accepted into the university. A student's mental health issues or other disabilities cannot be a consideration of acceptance into a college or university.

» An IEP or a 504 plan in high school does not guarantee disability services.

» Most colleges require that students with physical, medical, learning and neurodevelopmental disorders apply for disabilities services to get accommodations such as extended time for exams, a reduced course load, or academic support.

» If the mental health issues do not appear until college, a student can still apply for services, but typically he or she will first need to be evaluated.

» All students are required to meet the school's academic standards.

» Some colleges, such as Marshall University and Pace University, offer special programs for students with ASD.

How you can help

• Make the school's mental health services a primary factor in evaluating potential colleges. Before applying, research the services the mental health center provides; the training, credentials and expertise of its staff; and their availability for working with students on the Spectrum. When visiting campuses, stop by the student health clinic and inquire about their services.

- Find out if your child could see a school or private therapist who has expertise in working with students on the Spectrum; or go to the campus resource centers that help students with academics, organization, and planning, such as the Schwab Foundation centers.

- Help your child see that getting services is a private process; it is not shared with other students. Remind your child that ultimately it will be up to them to get the type of support they think would help them.

- If your child welcomes your participation, ask him or her to sign permission for the staff to contact you if they are concerned about your child. The mental health professionals cannot disclose what they talk about with your child without specific consent. Ask your child to give the education support center the same type of permission.

Chapter 7

Lessons Learned and Looking Forward

By now you should be well-versed in the challenges for ASD college students. You know that college is difficult for all students. However, it carries unique trials for ASD students who still have limited, though growing, options for support.

Indeed, there are more options for ASD students than ever before. While this is promising, it is not enough. Too many ASD students still suffer from a lack of appropriate support programs and services. Parents, therapists, doctors, and educators need to work together to increase understanding of ASD, and to build viable programs so more ASD students can have greater opportunities in higher education and beyond.

To build better support programs and services will require a different approach than we have pursued to date. Traditional campus mental health systems provide disability services only for those who struggle academically. However, many students on the Spectrum do well in school, struggling instead with interpersonal skills and the many practical issues of daily life.

Fortunately, there are increasing insights into the needs of students on the Spectrum. In the book *Student Mental Health: A Guide for Psychiatrists, Psychologists, and Leaders Serving in Higher Education*, by Lawrence Fung (2018), a child psychiatrist, notes that most clinicians who see college students on the Spectrum received their training in ASD during a child psychiatry fellowship. In effect, ASD is seen as a child disorder even though it often appears for the first time in high-functioning teens, college students, and adults. Fung acknowledges the need for a systems program that supports the students at the academic, social, communicative, and organizational levels.

Moving toward a systems approach

Fung's conclusion, plus the insights presented by several of the professionals cited in this book, and my professional experience working with ASD students, support the need for a systems approach for students on the Spectrum. Specifically, I suggest the following steps to begin that shift.

1. Recognize college students with ASD.

   College students with ASD need to be recognized as a growing population on campuses and should be included in all mental health and wellbeing programs.

   The more understood and accepted ASD students feel, the better they will be able to focus on their school-work, develop friendships, and contribute to—and benefit from—the college experience.

2. Prioritize mental health and wellbeing.

   Mental health and wellbeing should be priorities for all higher education institutions. The university president, board, and administration need to make mental health issues, including ASD and learning differences, a priority. Far too often these issues are overlooked until a crisis occurs.

3. Simplify services.

The process of getting mental health and disabilities services needs to be simplified and accelerated. It is common for students to wait one to two months to learn if they have qualified or, as is often the case for ASD students, to learn that they have been rejected because their grades are too high.

Often when the ASD student does qualify, they have to inform their teachers, who probably are not educated about the strengths and challenges of students on the Spectrum. And the mental health services they do receive typically overlook their sensory, social and emotional needs (Sarrett 2018). The process would be overwhelming for any student, and is especially difficult for those who often have social challenges and are reluctant to identify themselves as having a disability.

4. Decentralize services to make them more accessible.

Decentralize mental health services to improve access and reduce the stigma associated with going to the mental health clinic for help. This could possibly be done in partnerships with organizations such as Bring Change to Mind and Active Minds.

5. Expand mental health education.

College professionals—including the deans, teachers, and RAs—need to be educated about growing mental health issues of students in their campus communities. They need to understand how to support students experiencing mental health challenges, and then build programs to educate the general student population. Regular presentations by informed speakers can be an effective way to bridge the information gap.

Fortunately, some students and faculty are speaking out about the shame they felt having a mental health breakdown on campus, a physical disability, a learning difference, or a neurodevelopmental disorder. This helps normalize their experiences while acknowledging the isolation and depression they felt when they were first diagnosed, while building greater awareness and understanding among administration, faculty, and students.

As with decentralizing mental health services, this educational outreach could also possibly be done in partnerships with organizations such as Bring Change to Mind and Active Minds.

6. Give political voice to ASD.

Politically active student organizations are refocusing support groups for students with disabilities into action-oriented support groups that are demanding a voice. The problem is that few students on the Spectrum participate in these groups. They often do not feel like they are welcomed because their issues are not visible. Yet, if they did participate they would realize that they have a lot in common with peers in a wheelchair or who are hearing impaired. Over time, with support and encouragement from ASD-aware faculty and friends, it is reasonable to assume that more ASD students will find their voice.

7. Offer internships to ASD students.

There is a growing demand for college graduates to have real-life work experience, the kind that is found through internships. Some colleges have programs to help students on the Spectrum to get internships, but more opportunities for ASD students are needed. This is an example of how colleges can integrate thinking about the student's life, not only on campus, but also after graduation.

8. Bridge the artificial divide between mental health issues and ASD.

Universities need to bridge the divide between students with mental health issues and students with ASD. The separation of services often leaves students on the Spectrum without access to mental health services. It is important to recognize that students on the Spectrum rarely seek help because of their primary diagnosis. They are more likely to seek help because of another symptom, particularly their feelings of social isolation and awkwardness that can lead to feelings of anxiety, depression, worthlessness, and suicidal ideation.

9. Rethink the approach.

Referring a student to the university clinic is not enough. These clinics are typically under-funded and under-staffed, making it difficult, if not impossible, for them to meet the growing mental health needs of today's students, including those on the Spectrum.

Instead the treatment of mental health and disabilities must become a core part of the academic planning. The process must include board members, administrators, deans, RAs, and teachers, as well as mental health and disability services, community mental health professionals, and community treatment providers.

A systems approach does not look at the student in isolation, and instead focuses on the students in conjunction with their family of origin; their relationships on campus with teachers, peers, their university clubs; and their social and political activities. Their involvement in the larger community includes volunteering in community-service programs; participation in different religious, political programs and civic organizations; and utilizing community medical and mental health services. This informs the treatment and support plan and ensures that the student is not seen in isolation.

10. Include ASD in research and support groups.

Because ASD is viewed as a neurodevelopmental disorder—not a mental health disorder—students on the Spectrum today are not included in many research studies and support groups. Specifically, they need to be included in:

- research on mental health issues for college students in addition to research specifically on ASD

- college courses on mental health issues and adult psychiatry training programs

- professional workshops on learning differences.

Also, ASD students should be part of the organizations working to eliminate the stigma associated with mental health issues and create more positive, supportive networks on campuses. Right now, key organizations, including Active Minds and Bring Change to Mind, do not include ASD as a key diagnosis on their websites.[1] Similarly, the Jed Foundation (2011), which provides an outstanding model for campus-wide intervention for the prevention of suicide and drug addiction, doesn't include ASD in its otherwise excellent mental health resource center.

---

1   www.activeminds.org
    www.bringchange2mind.org

11. Improve training.

Adult psychiatrists, psychologists, social workers, therapists and counselors must be trained how to treat ASD.

Today many students on the Spectrum are misdiagnosed because the clinician has had no training in Autism Spectrum Disorder. The ASD population is growing too fast to depend solely on child therapists to see teenagers through adulthood. In recent years I have received calls from increasing numbers of therapists who question whether a client could be on the Spectrum. I have also been contacted by adults whose previous therapist(s) did not identify this issue correctly or felt that it should not be considered when working with the adult.

ASD training should be added to medical, graduate and ongoing education curricula to ensure better, more timely diagnosis of ASD. The topic of Autism Spectrum Disorders needs be included in seminars on mental health issues with the goal of removing the stereotypes of the condition, and reduce the feeling of isolation ASD students often experience.

12. Develop solid re-entry programs.

Most students who drop out of school due to mental health issues such as depression or anxiety leave voluntarily. In contrast, students who share suicidal ideation or attempt suicide are typically forced to leave because of the risk to the school's reputation and the fear of legal liability. Expulsion is a lot easier than providing the in-depth services the students need.

It is up to the student to notify the school about their plans to re-enter. Schools might give the student an option such as a year off to decide what is best for them. Schools that don't have a re-entry program advise the student to seek off-site support. It is often not enough to have a student's psychiatrist recommend re-entry into college. Many schools require students who have made suicide threats or attempts to sign a waiver that absolves the school from responsibility if the student attempts suicide again. Even when the student signs the form, many schools discourage them from returning.

Some students choose to go to a smaller school closer to home, a community college, or a therapeutic program that helps them develop better independent living skills, a working understanding of their diagnosis and the type of treatment that works for them. A good number of these students never return to school, which can lead to feelings of helplessness about college and job opportunities.

Fortunately, some colleges are slowly developing special programs designed to help these bright students re-enter a college or university. Boston University provides such a program—NITEO,[2] which means 'thrive or bloom' in Latin (Thielking 2017)—as does The Fountain House with its College Re-Entry Program.[3]

The Boston University program is unique in that it is specifically designed to help students find more adaptive ways to thrive at a college campus. They work on the social and practical demands of living on campus. They address the roadblocks that the students may have encountered socially, and work to replace poor coping habits (such as escaping online) with more adaptive programs on campus (like the

---

2   https://cpr.bu.edu/living-well/college/programs/niteo
3   https://collegereentry.org

gym, the arts, campus clubs, and support groups). Their goal is to make the students better equipped to go to college, utilize resources effectively, find better ways to cope with their stress, and accept the fact that it is OK if their path is different from what they first expected.

The Aspen Network helps students make the transition from home to college if they returned home after a negative experience or expulsion. The students live with peers in "pods" where they develop daily living skills such as shopping, cooking, and cleaning. The students need to attend a community college or have a part-time job. The study room does not have online access so no-one can play online games or search the web.

The Friends Program graduates

I realize that you may be wondering about what became of the students who were interviewed for this book. Most of the information came from the students' parents since it is hard to reach these young adults while they are at school or work.

All the students experienced times of self-doubt and low self-esteem, which contributed to their feelings of anxiety and depression. However, they also showed progress in many areas of their lives. They described times of joy and accomplishment. All the older students who graduated went on to paid jobs or graduate schools.

For most, the transformative change was that they accepted some type of service. What varied were their attitudes about seeing a therapist and having a diagnosis. Those who were more accepting thrived. Those who predominantly relied on their parents for support had a bumpier road than those who learned to reach out to the resources both at and outside the college.

Here are some specific updates:

- Steve, who resisted seeing a therapist during college and depended instead on his mother for support, began seeing a therapist for his anxiety. Today Steve is a librarian at a public institution.

- Sarah is still enjoying her dance troupe. She feels it has boosted her self-confidence, communication skills, and executive functioning. After all, she has had to be well-organized to handle their frequent performances and travels. Sarah plans to go to college and possibly study nursing.

- After resisting any academic support at college, Gabe registered for disability services and reduced his academic load. He loves participating in the marching band, is studying business, and has expanded his coursework beyond computer science and math to include a history class. He communicates with his psychologist and psychiatrist when needed.

- Thomas, who had considered suicide, turned his life around after a residential program in the Philippines. He was valedictorian of his high school class, and spoke about being on the Spectrum in his valedictorian address. He is now attending graduate school in religion on the other side of the country from his family. He has had an up-and-down experience at graduate school, because developing friendships and social communication remain difficult for him.

- Mandy, who told her son that it was all right to drop a class or two if the workload was overwhelming, said her son turned down the extra tutoring the school had offered. The next year he asked for extended test time, a step towards not viewing support as an insult to his abilities.

- One student, who was dismissed from college because he refused the services the school offered and instead played computer games, is now in a program for students who have not been able to make the transition to college. The goal is to foster autonomy and social skills. He has roommates, household responsibilities and shared dinners, and is required to have a job (paid or volunteer) or attend a community college. The program underlines the importance of mastering the daily living skills outlined in Chapter 3.

A special message to parents

Parents have shared with me how lonely many of them felt in this journey. Most of them turned to their spouse, a friend who had similar experiences, or their religion for support.

I hope that this book helps you understand that you are not alone. Many other parents are dealing with the same issues. If you are lonely, remember that you can contact the therapist who initially saw your child. If possible, connect with other parents of children on the Spectrum.

My hat is off to all of you who have worked so hard and given so much. Your work has changed the trajectory of your child's life.

What's more, you have helped countless other students on the Spectrum and their families as you have helped build understanding of ASD.

Please share your stories—together we can build greater awareness and new options for all ASD college students.

References

American Psychiatric Association (2013) *Diagnostic and Statistical Manual of Mental Health Disorders: DSM-5* (5th Ed.). Arlington, VA: American Psychiatric Association.

Autism Speaks (n.d.) *Associated Medical Conditions.* Autism Speaks. Accessed on 3/15/19 at www.autismspeaks.org/associated-medical-conditions-0

Bronfenbrenner, U. (1981) *The Ecology of Human Development.* Cambridge, MA: Harvard University Press.

Center for Collegiate Mental Health (CCMH) (2016) *2016 Annual Report.* University Park, PA: Penn State University. Accessed in 2017 at https://safesupportivelearning.ed.gov/resources/center-collegiate-mental-health-2016-annual-report

Child Mind Institute (2016) 'Going to college with autism'. Child Mind Institute. Accessed on 12/1/17 at www.childmind.org/article/going-to-college-with-autism

Cornish, P.A., Benton, S., Berry, G., Barros-Gomes, P. *et al.* (2017) 'Meeting the mental health needs of today's college student: reinventing services through Stepped Care 2.0.' *Psychological Services 14,* 4, 428–442.

Culpin, I., Mars, B., Pearson, R.M., Golding, J. *et al.* (2018) 'Autistic traits and suicidal thoughts, plans and self-harm in late adolescence: population-based cohort study.' *Journal of the American Academy of Child & Adolescent Psychiatry 57,* 5, 313–320.

Drug Policy Alliance (2019) 'Good Samaritan Fatal Overdose Prevention Laws.' Drug Policy Alliance. Accessed on 23/10/19 at www.drugpolicy.org/issues/good-samaritan-fatal-overdose-prevention-laws

Ehmke, R. (2019) *How using social media affects teenagers.* New York: Child Mind Institute. Accessed on 9/3/19 at www.childmind.org/article/how-using-social-media-affects-teenagers

Fung, L. (2018) 'Autism Spectrum Disorder.' In L.W. Roberts (ed.) *Student Mental Health: a Guide for Psychiatrists, Psychologists, and*

Leaders Serving in Higher Education. New York: American Psychiatric Association Publishing.

Gelbar, N.W., Shefcyk, A. and Riechow, B. (2015) 'A comprehensive survey of current and former college students with autism spectrum disorders.' *Yale Journal of Biology and Medicine 88*, 2593–2606.

Hamblet, E.C. (2011) 7 *Things to Know About College Disability Services*. New York: Understood. Accessed on 10/29/2019 at https://www.understood.org/en/school-learning/choosing-starting-school/leaving-high-school/7-things-to-know-about-college-disability-services

Hamblet, E.C. (2014) 'What parents and students with disabilities should know about college.' *Newspaper of the National Association of School Psychologists 42*, 5, 1–5.

Hamblet, E.C. (n.d.) *Successful transitions to college for students with disabilities*. Arlington, VA: Council for Exceptional Children. Accessed at www.cec.sped.org/News/Special-Education-Today/Need-to-Know/Need-to-Know-Successful-Transitions-to-College-for-Students-with-Disabilities

Hibbs, J. and Rostain, A. (2019) *The Stressed Years of Their Lives: Helping Your Kid Survive and Thrive During Their College Years*. New York: St. Martin's Press.

Hinshaw, S. (2017) *Another Kind of Madness: A Journey Through the Stigma and Hope of Mental Illness*. New York: St. Martin's Press.

Hinshaw, S. (2017) *The stigma around mental illness is its own kind of madness*. Vice. Accessed on 13/9/17 at www.vice.com/en_us/article/9k57ez/the-stigma-around-mental-illness-is-its-own-kind-of-madness

Jackson, S.L.J., Hart, L., Thierfeld Brown, J.T. and Volkmar, F. R. (2018) 'Brief report: self-reported academic, social, and mental health experiences of post-secondary students with Autism Spectrum Disorder.' *Journal of Autism Developmental Disorder 48*, 3, 643–650.

Jed Foundation Campus MHAP (2011) *A Guide to Campus Mental Health Action Planning*. New York: The Jed Foundation. Accessed on 12/2/14 at www.jedfoundation.org/wp-content/uploads/2016/07/campus-mental-health-action-planning-jed-guide.pdf

Ketchen Lipson, S., Gaddis, S.M., Heinze, J., Beck, K., and Eisenberg, D. (2015) 'Variations in student mental health and treatment utilization across U.S. colleges and universities.' *Journal of American College Health, 63*, 6, 388–396.

Leventhal-Belfer, L. (2013) 'Potential ramifications of DSM-5 classifications of Autistic Disorders: comments from a clinician's perspective.' *Journal of Autism and Developmental Disorders 43*, 3, 749–50.

LeViness, P., Bershad, C., and Gorman, K. (2017) *The Association of University and College Counseling Center Directors Annual Survey.* Reporting period: July 1, 2016 through June 30, 2017. Accessed on 2/19/18 at https://www.aucccd.org/assets/2017%20aucccd%20 survey-public-apr17.pdf

Lipari, R. and Jean-Francois, B. (2016) *The CBHSQ short report. A day in the life of college students aged 18–22: substance use facts.* Research Triangle Park: Substance Abuse and Mental Health Services Administration (SAMHSA). Accessed on 5/20/19 at www.samhsa. gov/data/sites/default/files/report_2361/ShortReport-2361.html

Mattila M-L., Hurtig T., Haapsamo H., Jussila, K. *et al.* (2010) 'Comorbid psychiatric disorders associated with Asperger Syndrome/high functioning autism: a community- and clinic-based study.' *Journal of Autism and Developmental Disorders 40, 9,* 1080–93.

Meeks, L. and Masterson, T.L. (2016) *Parties, Dorms, and Social Norms: A Crash Course in Safe Living for Young Adults on the Autistic Spectrum.* London: Jessica Kingsley Publishers.

National Alliance on Mental Illness (2012) *College students speak: a survey report on mental health.* NAMI. Accessed on 5/8/17 at https://www. nami.org/About-NAMI/Publications-Reports/Survey-Reports/ College-Students-Speak_A-Survey-Report-on-Mental-H.pdf

National Institute on Alcohol Abuse and Alcoholism (NIAAA) (2015) 'Fall Semester—A Time for Parents to Discuss the Risks of College Drinking.' NIAAA. Updated August 2019. Accessed on 23/10/19 at https://www.niaaa.nih.gov/publications/brochures-and-fact-sheets/ time-for-parents-discuss-risks-college-drinking

Pace University (n.d.) *OASIS College Support Program.* www.pace.edu/oasis

Riba, M., Kirsch, D., Martel, A. and Goldsmith, M. (2015) 'Preparing and training the college mental health workforce.' *Academy of Psychiatry 39, 5,* 498–502.

Roberts, L.W. (2018) *Student Mental Health: A Guide for Psychiatrists, Psychologists, and Leaders Serving in Higher Education.* New York: American Psychiatric Association Publishing.

Sarrett, J.C. (2018) 'Autism and accommodations in higher education: insights from the autism community.' *Journal of Autism and Developmental Disorders 48, 3,* 679–693.

Siegel, D. (2013) *Brainstorm: The Power and Purpose of the Teenage Brain.* New York: Penguin Group.

Selkie, E.M., Fales, J.L., and Moreno, M.A. (2016) 'Cyberbullying prevalence among US middle and high school-aged adolescents: a systematic review and quality assessment.' *Journal of Adolescent Health* 58, 2, 125–133.

Steiner-Adair, C. and Barker, T.H. (2013) *The Big Disconnect: Protecting Childhood and Family Relationships in the Digital Age*. New York: Harper Business.

The Mayo Clinic (2018) 'Alcohol use disorder.' The Mayo Clinic. Accessed on 23/10/19 at https://www.mayoclinic.org/diseases-conditions/alcohol-use-disorder/symptoms-causes/syc-20369243

Thielking, M. (2017) 'A semester-long program aims to help college students with mental health conditions.' *Scientific American, 21 December, 2017.* Accessed on 2/26/18 at www.scientificamerican.com/article/a-semester-long-program-aims-to-help-college-students-with-mental-health-conditions

US Department of Education (2019) *Family Educational Rights and Privacy Act (FERPA)*, US Department of Education. Accessed on 4/10/19 at Studentprivacy.ed.gov/topic/family-educational-rights-privacy-act-ferpa

van den Eijnden, R.J., Spijkerman, R., Vermulst, A.A., van Rooij, T.J., and Engels, R.C. (2010) 'Compulsive internet use among adolescents: bidirectional parent-child relationships.' *Journal of Abnormal Child Psychology 38*, 1, 77–89.

Walker, C.M., Sockman, B.R., and Koehn, S. (2011) 'An exploratory study of cyberbullying with undergraduate university students.' *TechTrends* 55, 2, 31–38.

White, A. and Hingson, R. (2013) 'The burden of alcohol use: excessive alcohol consumption and related consequences among college students.' *Alcohol Research 35*, 2, 201–18.

White, D., Hillier, A., Frye, A., and Makrez, E. (2019) 'College students' knowledge and attitudes towards students on the autism spectrum.' *Journal of Autism and Developmental Disorders 49*, 5, 2699–2705.

White, S.W., Ollendick, T.H., and Bray, B.C. (2011) 'College students on the autism spectrum: prevalence and associated problems.' *Autism* 15, 6, 683–701.

Yuhas, D. (2019) *Untangling the ties between autism and obsessive-compulsive disorder*. Spectrum. Accessed on 4/28/19 at www.spectrumnews.org/features/deep-dive/untangling-ties-autism-obsessive-compulsive-disorder

Zupanick, C.E. (2014) *The New DSM-5: Anxiety Disorders And Obsessive-Compulsive Disorders*. Accessed on 1/6/17 at www.mentalhelp.net/articles/the-new-dsm-5-anxiety-disorders-and-obsessive-compulsive-disorders

Further Reading

Best Colleges (n.d.) *College Guide for Students with Psychiatric Disabilities.* Best Colleges. Accessed on 2/26/18 at www.bestcolleges.com/resources/college-planning-with-psychiatric-disabilities

Best Practices for Mental Health Services in Colleges and Universities. Accessed at www.okhighered.org/campus-safety/resources/CBP-mental-best-practices-higher-ed.pdf

Bring Change to Mind, www.bringchange2mind.org

Centers for Disease Control and Prevention (n.d.) *Facts About CDC's Autism and Developmental Disabilities Monitoring (ADDM) Network.* CDC. Accessed at www.cdc.gov/ncbddd/autism/materials/addm-factsheet.html

Centers for Disease Control and Prevention (2018) *Autism prevalence slightly higher in CDC's ADDM Network.* CDC. Accessed at www.cdc.gov/media/releases/2018/p0426-autism-prevalence.html

Center for Mental Health Services (U.S.) (2007) *Building bridges: mental health on campus: student mental health leaders and college administrators, counselors, and faculty in dialogue.* Rockville, MD:US Dept. of Health and Human Services, Substance Abuse and Mental Health Administration, Center for Mental Health Services.

Gardiner, E. and Iarocci, G. (2014) 'Students with autism spectrum disorder in the university context: peer acceptance predicts intention to volunteer.' *Journal of Autism and Developmental Disorders 44,* 5, 1008–1017.

The Jed Foundation, www.jedfoundation.org

Jed Campus, www.jedcampus.org

The Suicide Prevention Resource Center (n.d.) *Colleges and Universities.* Waltham, MA: SPRC. Accessed at www.sprc.org/settings/colleges-universities

Winerman, L. (2017) 'By the numbers: stress on campus.' *American Psychological Association 48*, 8, 88.

Zeldovich, L. (2018) *The evolution of "autism" as a diagnosis, explained.* Spectrum. Accessed at www.spectrumnews.org/news/evolution-autism-diagnosis-explained

College programs attuned to needs of college students on the autism spectrum

Autism Speaks (n.d.) 'A Retrospective on Postsecondary Educational Opportunities: An interview with Ruth Christ Sullivan, Ph.D., founder, West Virginia Autism Training Center, Marshall University.' *Postsecondary Educational Opportunities Guide.* Autism Speaks. Accessed at www.autismspeaks.org/family-services/tool-kits/postsecondary

Marshall University, *The College Program for Students with Autism Spectrum Disorder.* Huntington, WV: Marshall University. Accessed at www.marshall.edu/collegeprogram

Borrell, B. (2018) 'How colleges can prepare for students with autism.' Spectrum. Accessed at www.spectrumnews.org/features/deep-dive/colleges-can-prepare-students-autism

Pace University (n.d.) *OASIS College Support Program.* New York: Pace University. Accessed at www.pace.edu/oasis

Autism Speaks (n.d.) *Postsecondary Educational Opportunities Guide.* Autism Speaks. Accessed at www.autismspeaks.org/tool-kit/postsecondary-educational-opportunities-guide

Friendship Circle (n.d.) *Spotlight: 10 Colleges with Programs for ASD Students.* West Bloomfield, MI: Friendship Circle. Accessed at www.friendshipcircle.org/blog/2016/07/22/spotlight-10-colleges-with-programs-for-asd-students

Thrive College Counseling: Marci Schwartz, Ph.D., independent educational consultant, works with students with unique learning needs to find their best college fit, www.thrivecollegecounseling.com

Navigating college

Brown, J.T., Wolf, L.E., King, L., and Kukiela Bork, G.R. (2012) *The Parent's Guide to College for Students on the Autism Spectrum*. Shawnee Mission, KS: AAPC Publishing.

The Autistic Self Advocacy Network (ASAN) (2011) *Navigating College: A handbook on self-advocacy written for autistic students from autistic adults*. ASAN: The Autistic Self Advocacy Network. Accessed at www.navigatingcollege.org

Disclosing the diagnoses with your child

Mitchell, L. (n.d.) *It's not a secret: Why disclosure is important*. Asperger/ Autism Network (AANE). www.aane.org/not-secret-disclosure-important

Borrell, B. (2018) 'How colleges can prepare for students with autism.' Spectrum. Accessed at www.spectrumnews.org/features/deep-dive/colleges-can-prepare-students-autism

Hamblet, E.C. (2014) 'What parents and students with disabilities should know about college.' *Communiqué 42*, 5. www.ldadvisory.com/wp-content/uploads/NASP_WhatParentsandStudents.pdf

College Autism Network, www.CollegeAutismNetwork.org

Student support groups

Most of these groups work with students in high school and on college campuses. However, they do not list autism on their sites as a mental health disorder. They do include many of the disorders that are common for students on the Spectrum, including anxiety, depression, and ADHD. I have contacted them to encourage them to include ASD, but the stereotype gets in the way. I encourage readers to check them out for students who have similar issues.

- Active Minds: student-run support groups for peers with mental health issues on high schools and college campuses. www.activeminds.org

- Bring Change 2 Mind: the goal of their program is to educate students about mental health disorders, foster support groups, and advocate for the normalization of mental health disorders. www.bringchange2mind.org

- The Jed Foundation: a not-for-profit organization whose goal is to promote students' wellbeing and prevent suicide. www. jedfoundation.org

- The Jed Foundation's Mental Health Resource Center: expert information and resources to help teens and young adults navigate common emotional health issues, learn how they can support each other, and overcome common challenges as they journey to adulthood. The resource also lists guidelines for what to do if they are concerned about a friend or themselves. www.jedfoundation. org/mental-health-resource-center

Starting the conversation about college and your mental health

The Columbia Lighthouse Project (n.d.) *Identify Risk. Prevent Suicide.* The Columbia Lighthouse Project. Accessed at www.cssrs.columbia.edu

Lipari, R. and Beda J-F. (2016) 'A Day in the Life of College Students Aged 18-22 Substance Use Facts.' *The CBHSQ Report.* Research Triangle Park: SAMHSA. Accessed at www.samhsa.gov/data/sites/default/files/report_2361/ShortReport-2361.html

Peer-support programs for college students on the Spectrum

A growing number of universities attuned to the needs of college students on the Spectrum have developed their own peer-support programs. Parents should look at the colleges of interest to see how they address this issue.

Wrong Planet (www.wrongplanet.net)

This is a web community designed for individuals (and their parents and professionals working with them) with autism, Asperger's Syndrome, ADHD, PDDs, and other neurological differences. The website provides a discussion forum where members communicate with each other, an article section with exclusive articles and how-to guides, a blog feature, and more.

Peer-Support Programs—Indiana Institute on Disability and Community (www.iidc.indiana.edu/pages/Peer-Support-Programs)

This program helps build cross-age peer/buddy support by assigning older students to help a student with ASD with classroom activities.

Donevan, C. (2017) 'Navigating Life on Campus When You're on the Autism Spectrum.' *All Things Considered*. National Public Radio, Inc. (npr), 28 November 2017. (www.npr.org/201711/28/566788182/navigating-life-on-campus-when-you-are-on-the-autism-spectrum)

Child Mind Institute (2016) *Going to College with Autism*. New York: Child Mind Institute. Accessed on 12/1/17 at www.childmind.org/article/going-to-college-with-autism

Hoffman, J. (2016) 'Along the Autism Spectrum, a Path Through Campus Life.' *The New York Times*, 19 November, 2016. (www.nytimes.com/2016/11/20/health/autism-spectrum-college.html)

Job placement opportunities for college graduates on the Spectrum

Andy Aczel's program helps facilitate individuals' transition to a work site by providing supervision at all levels of the program; the mental health staff, the CEO, the head of the students team, and their colleagues. Andy Aczel, andy@specialistguild.org

Bernick, M. (2019) 'The Autism Community Focuses on Jobs, Not Grievances.' *Wall Street Journal*, 6 January, 2019. Accessed on 2/4/19 at www.wsj.com/articles/the-autism-community-focuses-on-jobs-not-grievances-11546646862

Dominus, S. (2019) 'The future of work. Open office: What happens when people who have trouble fitting into a traditional workplace get one designed just for them.' *New York Times*, 21 February, 2019. Accessed on 2/21/19 at www.nytimes.com/interactive/2019/02/21/magazine/autism-office-design.html

Eng, D. (2018) 'Where autistic workers thrive.' *Fortune*, 24 June, 2018. Accessed on 2/4/19 at www.fortune.com/18/06/24/where-autistic-workers-thrive

Oesch, T. (2017) *Autism at work: Hiring and training employees on the Spectrum*. Raleigh, NC: Workforce Development. Accessed on 2/4/18 at www.trainingindustry.com/articles/workforce-development/autism-at-work-hiring-and-training-employees-on-the-spectrum

Pesce, N. (2017) *Most college grads with autism can't find jobs. This group is fixing that.* MarketWatch. Accessed on 12/14/18 at www.marketwatch.com/story/most-college-grads-with-autism-cant-find-jobs-this-group-is-fixing-that-2017-04-10-5881421

Preston, E. (2016) *Work in progress: An inside look at autism's job boom.* Spectrum. Accessed on 2/4/19 at www.spectrumnews.org/.../work-in-progress-an-inside-look-at-autisms-job-boom

Stanford Medicine (2019) *Stanford Neurodiversity Project: Building Alliances on Campus.* Stanford, CA: Stanford Medicine. Accessed on 1/4/19 at www.med.stanford.edu/neurodiversity.html

Index